Dementi Sexuailiy

The rose that never wilts

ELAINE WHITE

Foreword by Professor Mary Marshall

Hawker Publications

Dementia and Sexuality: A rose that never wilts

First published in 2011 by
Hawker Publications Ltd,
Culvert House, Culvert Road,
London SW11 5DH
Tel: 020 7720 2108
www.careinfo.org

British Library Cataloguing in Publication Data
A catalogue record for this book is available from the British Library

ISBN 9781874790976

Copy edited by Kate Hawkins
Designed by Andrew Chapman, www.preparetopublish.com
Set in the Museo family

Printed and bound in Great Britain by Information Press Ltd, Oxford

Hawker Publications also publishes the
Journal of Dementia Care and *Caring Times*.

Contents

*This book is dedicated in loving memory of my husband
and soul mate, John Alwyne White,
who died 21st May, 1979.*

Acknowledgments

I would like to express my gratitude and thanks to my mentor Emeritus Professor Mary Marshall for her constant support, feedback, constructive criticism, enthusiasm and confidence in my ability to write this book. I am also extremely thankful to Marti Blanch, who so willingly shared her knowledge and originally inspired me to think about sexuality, not just as a physical act but in broader terms with all the intricacies encompassed by the terminology.

I would like to acknowledge the special people living with dementia who continually challenged me to look beyond their diagnosis and to understand why their dementia damaged brain caused them to express their sexuality in the way that was often perceived by care staff as inappropriate. Unfortunately, they and their family members who so generously shared so much information have to remain anonymous but having the opportunity to problem-solve the complexities of their situations taught me so much.

My special thanks to Ann Moylan, Fran Dumont, Diana Golvers and June Morris for their valuable suggestions and guidance when I needed another opinion. I am especially grateful to my granddaughter, Hilary, who came up with the title "A rose that never wilts" which proved so apt. I am grateful to Richard Hawkins for his feedback, encouragement, patience and guidance on the structure and content of this book, and to Kate Hawkins for her editing.

Finally I would like to especially acknowledge and thank my family, Sue, Iain, Peter and Kerrie, who are always there for me, with their continual support, assistance and encouragement, and also for their faith in my ability to write this book; without them I don't think I could have completed it.

Foreword
by Professor Mary Marshall

The 2007 Alzheimer's Australia annual conference in Perth was a really splendid conference with lots of excellent speakers and some very interesting parallel sessions. One of the best was Elaine White talking about challenging sexual behaviour, the focus being mainly care homes. I was instantly engaged by her quiet authority. She is a very experienced nurse who has worked for many years, as both a trainer and a consultant, helping staff to try to understand the sexual needs of people with dementia. She is perfectly comfortable and confident in addressing this topic and is convinced that, with some knowledge of the brain damage of dementia, and a thorough understanding of the people concerned and of their behaviour, a resolution can be found in most instances. Her paper to the conference session was illuminated by stories from her practice in a way that was totally convincing. When we were talking after the session, I suggested to her that she really ought to write a book because there is so little material in this area of dementia care. She agreed and I put her in touch with Richard Hawkins, founder of Hawker Publications. Richard was able to visit Elaine when he was in New South Wales to confirm the requirements of the book.

In the intervening time we have become great email friends as I have tried to give her the encouragement she needed as a new author. She came to the UK in 2009 to talk at the DSDC York conference and was able to spend some time with me in Edinburgh afterwards. My admiration increased all the time as she battled with all sorts of illnesses and accidents to complete the book.

The book is worth every ounce of encouragement from me and every ton of effort on her part. I think we have a really useful book here which will be of immense help to staff working in dementia care, and probably for relatives too. It is straightforward, well organised and based on real experience. The case studies are hugely helpful. The book is easy to read and free from jargon. She shares methods of analysis which she has found useful. I am really delighted to have played some small part in making it possible for Elaine's wisdom to reach a wide audience so it can benefit people with dementia everywhere.

Introduction

There are a lot of myths and misconceptions and negative attitudes regarding sexuality and dementia. Carers, both primary (spouse, partner and/or family members) and care staff, find a person living with dementia pursuing sexual desires and drives difficult to accept. There can be a great deal of embarrassment and carers, in general, may even feel these activities are rather off-putting, not knowing whether to discourage or support them.

My experience as a clinical nurse consultant in geriatrics and aged care education over the last 20 years has led me on a problem-solving journey to specialise in this subject. I realised early in my clinical position that few people in either of the caring roles, primary family carers or care staff, are equipped with the knowledge or skills to help the person living with dementia express their unmet sexual needs in an appropriate manner.

This book has been written with care staff in mind, those working in the acute care sector, community services or residential facilities, to give some practical guidelines which will enable the person living with dementia to express their sexuality in a positive way or address any complex or challenging perceived inappropriate sexual behaviour that may arise.

I have divided the book into three sections. "Setting the Scene", the first, explores the meaning of sexuality and its many component parts. It continues with a look at the issue of attitudes to old age generally. These may well be contributing factors to the myths and misconceptions that could hinder care. Similar attitudes and issues that frequently occur for same sex partners have been integrated throughout the book.

The section concludes by examining the disinhibition that arises when the process of dementia damages the frontal lobe of the brain, limiting the person's insight or awareness of social proprieties. The section also explores the impact of any overriding damage or dysfunction that may have occurred in the remaining cerebral lobes that may compromise the person's behaviour.

Primary carer/s have not been forgotten. Much of what has been written will relate to their situations within the home environment. However, I do acknowledge that the primary carer does have challenges perhaps not seen by care staff in an acute or residential setting. Therefore the second section "Sustaining Relationships" will include a chapter on these issues and how care staff can support and engage with the primary carer. A chapter describing a useful model of care to establish connections with embarrassed or worried primary carers has been incorporated into this section. Completing the section is a chapter on ethical dilemmas, exploring such questions as a person living with dementia's capacity to give 'decision-specific' consent to intimate sexual encounters.

The importance of education is highlighted throughout the various chapters to increase knowledge, skills, sensitivity and communication channels for both care staff and primary carers.

The last section of the book, "Discovering Solutions", includes a pathway designed to provide clarity to the process of identifying, diagnosing and solving perceived problems. This pathway emphasises the importance of obtaining both life and sexual histories for the person living with dementia. These histories are the basis upon which creative person-centred life-enhancing strategies are planned and implemented. They aim to assist the person living with dementia in expressing their sexuality appropriately at whatever level, direction or activity needed. Ways to rechannel the person's inappropriate behaviour to promote dignity and well being and a positive outcome are described.

To emphasise specific issues or situations and the strategies I have used to achieve a good outcome, I have described some of the many stories of people I have been asked to help. Identities have been changed to protect privacy but I am grateful to each of them and their families for the insight they have provided to me and, I hope, to you the reader.

The final chapter demonstrates that the challenges and complexities of facilitating change can be overcome by education. It will be shown

Dementia and Sexuality

that education is the key to promoting understanding that the person living with dementia is a vibrant sexual being in so many ways and will be until the day they die.

I acknowledge that some of my readers may not be comfortable with some of my descriptive text, and their own personal relationship experiences, cultural or religious beliefs may separate them or even alienate them from my problem solving strategies. I intend no offence but I need to stress that from my own clinical experience I have found my problem solving pathway to be effective. Through this process people have become more settled and happier living in their world of dementia. My purpose is for the reader to extract from the text a strategy that would be of value for a particular individual person's unmet sexual needs and, if this is achieved, then this book has been successful.

Elaine White, New South Wales, Australia, September 2010

PART ONE

Setting the Scene

*'Grow old along with me
The best is yet to be'*

Robert Browning

CHAPTER ONE

Defining Sexuality: What Does it Really Mean?

The purpose of this chapter is to facilitate the reader's understanding of sexuality in wider dimensions than as just a physical act. It is designed to describe sexuality in terms of a concept with its many different parts that all interconnect to form the broader intricacies and attitudes which make up human sexuality.

"Sexuality: a central aspect of being human throughout life and encompasses sex, gender, identities and roles, sexual orientation, eroticism, pleasure, intimacy and reproduction"

World Health Organisation (2006)

Dementia and Sexuality

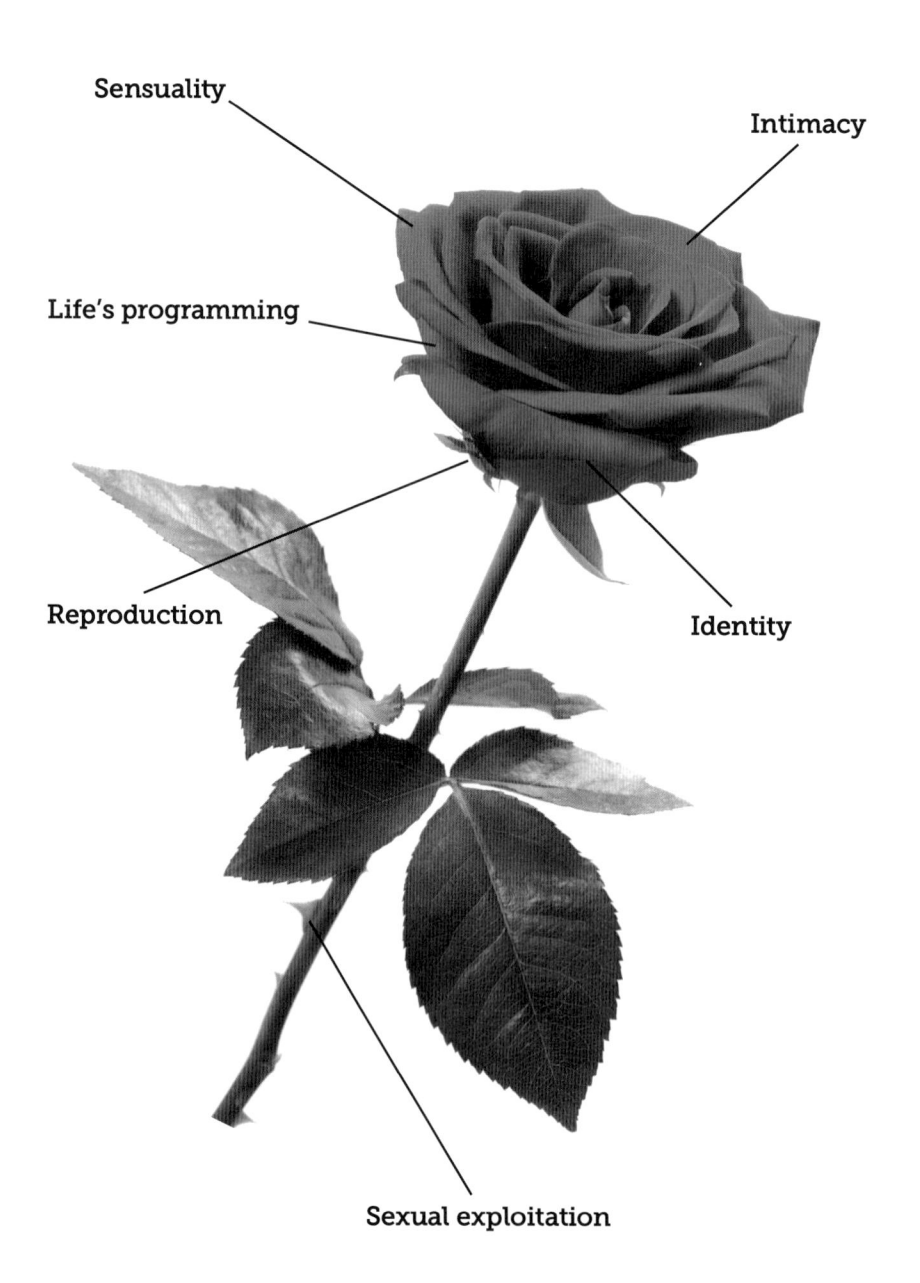

Sensuality

Intimacy

Life's programming

Reproduction

Identity

Sexual exploitation

For many people the term sexuality stimulates just two thought pathways. They either think of gender (male or female) or of sexuality as a purely physical activity between two people. However there is much more to this terminology. Blanch *et al* (1990) defined 'sexuality' in broader terms, for example, describing it as a concept depicted in the mind's eye in "terms of a beautiful flower".

I have expanded on Blanch *et al*'s flower image concept and, being more specific, seen it as a rosebud. When the magnificent rosebud unfurls, its petals reveal the many parts which make up 'sexuality', as follows:

- Sensuality
- Intimacy
- Identity
- Life programming
- Reproduction.

Following down the stem, unfortunately this beautiful rosebud has its thorny 'darker' side; the hidden parts that come under the cover of:

- Sexual exploitation.

Each part of the now open rose is like a piece of a jigsaw puzzle, linking together to form "the big picture" of human sexuality. How one addresses one's own sexuality will depend on either positive or negative experiences being stored within petals of the rose. To explain the intricacies of this concept, the contents of each petal will be described.

Sensuality
Sensuality is more than just gratification of our senses. It is how our brain, which controls our bodily senses, becomes aware, interprets, and responds to the five major senses that are the very core of oneself, one's very being:

- Smell
- Touch
- Taste
- Vision
- Hearing.

Dementia and Sexuality

Some individuals develop a preferred sense which influences how that person presents themselves to others; the essence of their bodily scent, the perfume they use, how a person communicates or how they dress to attract others. Some individuals may appear more sensuous or voluptuous than others; a female may choose to wear low cut dresses or short skirts, whereas a male might present himself in tight jeans or open fronted shirt. Of course this presentation of self is often influenced by whom one is likely to be with or who one is trying to attract.

Response to pleasurable stimuli varies from person to person, some get great pleasure out of the smell of a gardenia or perhaps someone else's perfume, whilst for others it might be the aroma of a roast dinner cooking or the salt spray as they walk along a beach enjoying the feel of the wind in their hair and the sand under their feet.

Pleasurable stimuli are many – seeing a beautiful sunset, a magnificent waterfall, the face of a loved one or hearing the birds in the rustling tree tops. For some a sensual experience can evolve via a candlelit dinner and mood-setting soft music. Their senses of sight and sound are stimulated but also taste with sumptuous food and drink such as good champagne, strawberries and chocolate.

Many people react to nice 'touchy-feely' things as well. The sensation of having your hair brushed by someone, the feel of velvet, silk or perhaps sleeping under satin sheets, sitting in a warm spa or having a body massage with nice smelling perfumed oil can be very pleasurable.

The sense of touch is powerful especially when it originates from kissing, holding, cuddling, fondling, caressing oneself or another person and it can often lead to the arousal of strong physical desires and drives. Some people satisfy the sensual side of their self by enjoying sensually stimulating erotic material, described by Nay (2004) as "explicit magazines and movies". These sensual desires and drives can progress into a passionate lovemaking union between two consenting individuals or self-gratification in the form of masturbation. Here sexuality moves into another part, the realm of intimacy.

Intimacy

The need for closeness and absence of loneliness is inherent in all of us; it is what drives an individual to seek a compatible intimate companion or 'soul mate'. Intimacy, as stated in Alzheimer's Australia, Vic. (2008), encompasses the sensuous "caring touch, giving and receiving loving warmth and affection, sharing feelings".

Moss *et al* (1993) describe intimacy as having five levels:

- Commitment: feelings of closeness, cohesion and connection
- Affective Intimacy: a deep sense of caring, compassion and positive regard
- Cognitive Intimacy: shared thinking about and an awareness of others, information, values and the goals of the relationship
- Physical Intimacy: sharing physical encounters ranging from proximity to sexual intercourse
- Mutuality: a process of exchange.

Whilst the first three levels described by Moss are self explanatory, for most people the fourth level of intimacy – sharing a physical intimate encounter – is not only the meeting of two bodies but a deep connecting emotional experience as well. As Greengross *et al* (1989) have explained, "the shared intimacy of body contact is more than genital excitement; it can offer reassurance, comfort and an opportunity to show love and tenderness, sharing joys and fears that are rarely spoken about in the cold light of day".

There does need to be an appreciation, however, that this might not be the case for every person. Sometimes physical intimacy can be an impersonal encounter, as explained by Nay (2004): "relieving one's sexual frustration with a sex worker". Such encounters can bring their own personal sexual gratifications and satisfaction.

Mutuality, on the other hand, Moss *et al*'s fifth level of intimacy, is best described as mutual respect and trust. The presence of trust can generate feelings of safety and security in a relationship, also comfort

Dementia and Sexuality

and solace; 'a shoulder to lean on' during times of grief or when other problems arise.

Mutuality also includes special feelings of ease and bodily desire in order to reveal and share oneself with another person. For example, an older couple sharing a life together, respecting each other, appreciating what gives one another pleasure and what leads to physical sexual arousal and satisfaction, have no inhibitions about their ageing bodies. With such an established mutual intimate relationship and a developed sexual freedom, post menopause, physical sexual activity becomes a natural part of their shared lives.

Kuhn's (2002) research found "the need for intimacy probably lasts until the end of life". Therefore, it does need to be appreciated that a death of a partner can leave a huge sexual as well as emotional gap in a person's life. As a consequence some individuals will have a need to seek alternative intimate opportunities.

Identity

Identify is what the whole 'concept of sexuality' revolves around: the individual's identity, the 'who' the person is. Bancroft (2009) states "it involves the whole experience of self; feelings of self-esteem, relationships with others, roles that we take on or have been given". Therefore as a person grows older it is also important to recognise the 'who' they have been over their entire life cycle.

Whether an individual is male or female, heterosexual, homosexual, bisexual, transsexual or transvestite, an older person has had a lot of life experiences. They may have a variety of pathways and roles; roles explained by White (2010), such as:

- Son/daughter, grandchild and sibling
- Friend, student, employee and colleague
- Boyfriend/girlfriend, lover, fiancé and spouse/partner
- Parent, neighbour, citizen, confidant, grandparent and senior citizen.

These roles become interwoven as the person steps in and out of them as time goes by. Nay *et al* (2007) explain that people also have "histories, contexts, families, goals and strengths". There are also religious and cultural beliefs as well as varying personality traits that shape the person's true identity. The social exposure, experiences, achievements, disappointments and wisdom gained along the way and the impact they have had on others are what contribute to making up the sum of the 'who' the person is.

"Since sexual identity," according to Hajjar *et al* (2004), "is closely interwoven with one's concept of self-worth, denying sexuality can deleteriously affect not only one's sex life, but also self-image, social relationships and mental health."

Appearance is an important way a person establishes their identity and also their personality in the outside world. Factors include grooming — getting one's hair done, nails manicured, make-up on, for the females perhaps, while males may like to be clean shaven with shoes shined. Dress, demeanour, deportment, preferred choice of colour, food, lifestyle, as well as physical sexual preference all contribute.

In many cases an individual's chosen career e.g. teacher, carpenter, nurse, accountant creates their working life identity. Even when retired, this past identity remains as an integral part of their persona, and will continue to be part of the person's identity to the day they die.

In the same way, for the individual who has always considered themselves to be a bit of a 'lover' and has had a sustained physically active sexual life then the desire to continue to pursue these activities remains part of the *who' the person is*, even in older age or with a diagnosis of dementia, despite what younger people may think. Fondling, caressing, kissing, sharing oneself with another, giving and receiving pleasure not only intertwines both concepts of 'sensuality' and 'intimacy' but can continue to enhance the person's identity of *'who' they still are.*

Dementia and Sexuality

Life's programming

Where and how sexual information was gathered during their life has a big bearing on an individual's attitude, and perception of, sexual behaviour. To appreciate how either positive or negative attitudes to sexual behaviour have developed, each care staff member needs to reflect on their own adolescent days and remember the origins of their sexual education:

- Was it from parents, siblings, friends or through the school education programme?
- Were parents always comfortable talking about the 'facts of life' or did they project negative vibes?
- Did mother and father send out different messages?
- What moral standards and beliefs did parents have?
- What examples did parents set?
- Was sexual information gathered from sniggering whispers, innuendos or snide remarks made from behind the school toilets?
- Did the sexual information come from the media, reading books and magazines or watching movies?
- Were there any biases from religious or cultural beliefs?
- Were there community biases or prejudices on such issues as sex before marriage, abortions, single mothers, same sex or bisexual partners, transgender people or transvestites?
- Were there any unwanted sexual advances, particularly at a young age?

For some, sex education can start early. It is a common occurrence for younger girls and boys to do their own exploring such as, "Show me yours and I'll show you mine". So much depends on how human sexuality is shown, how accurate, how natural it is described.

If human sexuality is shown as being part of a loving and respectful lasting relationship between two people, positive attitudes develop. Unfortunately, however, negative attitudes can form if sexuality is treated as a taboo subject, mysterious, something to be hidden or simply something one did to have children.

It must also be appreciated that culturally and linguistically diverse backgrounds can influence the way sexuality is viewed and expressed. These influences should always be taken into account when sexuality is an issue.

In recent times young people have been brought up on 'stranger danger' alerts; teachers cannot touch children any more, there are no more comfort hugs in the playground or classroom if a child is hurt. While the reasons for this caution are understandable, the danger is that this message might eventually lead to a reluctance to touch someone or accept a touch or to form a close relationship.

Divorce rates are increasing so some children may see their parents with many different partners. With only this example before them, some children, as they become young adults, may only seek short-term relationships or even 'one-night stands' where the only requirement is the use of condoms or the Pill, and no other personal attachments are necessary. Indeed sex may be considered by some young people as the normal way to end an evening out. The trouble is that if there is no respect within a relationship, no endearment, then physical sexual activity alone can eventually lead to disdain.

Many young people think that they only, in their life cycle, invented physical sex! How wrong that is! Nevertheless it may make the thought of older people having physical sexual activity rather appalling to them. Hopefully, however, with a growing awareness of the needs of older people, young people will eventually come to realise, as the noted author and poet Somerset Maugham once wrote, "Old age has its pleasures which though different, are no less than the pleasures of youth".

Reproduction

I acknowledge that human reproduction is a very important part of the big picture of human sexuality. However, discussion on it has been omitted from the book, not because of its unimportance but because the older person has usually moved beyond the reproductive side of life. Their focus is now on maintaining all the intricacies of sexuality and intimate connections that will contribute to their sense of well being and enhance their quality of living.

Dementia and Sexuality

Sexual exploitation

Sexual exploitation is unfortunately the thorny, darker part of the rose. It includes such illegal acts as pornography, incest, paedophilia, rape, sexual abuse, sexual slavery and torture. Some cultures continue to practice female circumcision, which is against the beliefs of many other cultures and thus deemed to be female genital mutilation. It is not surprising that throughout our lifetime we develop prejudices and negative attitudes towards these heinous activities.

In recent years more people are coming forward to tell their story of childhood sexual abuse. Often these stories have been hidden for many years. Incest, paedophilia or exposing children to pornographic material has been practised by predators, frequently in a position of trust. They have been family members, friends, or even a parent's live-in partner. The predator may also be a trusted member of the clergy or youth group as recent court cases and media exposure have revealed. It seems to be commonplace that the predator asks the young children or teenagers to keep the sexual activity a secret from their parent/parents. Over time feelings of guilt and shame build up in the child's psyche leaving long lasting psychological damage.

Rape, on the other hand, is violent, a denigration of another person's body and is certainly a police matter. Rape does not stop with younger people. Police records indicate rape atrocities have occurred to frail older people, people living with dementia or disability. The perpetrator is often found to be a person in a position of trust (O'Neill, 2006). Feelings of devastation, aversion and repugnance are left behind. Commonly the victim reports feeling dehumanised and devalued as a person. Nay (2007) states "the victim can feel dirty, guilty, depressed and unable to enjoy healthy sexual relationships". Similar feelings have been expressed by 'wartime comfort women', women forced into prostitution to work in military brothels during World War II. Once again a lot of psychological damage occurred.

Media releases during wartime, over the years, have alerted us to many instances of sexual violence, torture or other modes of human denigration. Sexual torture is frequently used as a form of power and control to degrade prisoners of war, as well as citizens of enemy occupied worn-torn countries much to the abhorrence of war crime tribunals. The lasting, haunting horrors of being the victim are unimaginable.

Inevitably how care staff view their own sexuality and those people in their care will depend on their attitudes, moral values and codes of conduct, all of which are influenced by their own life's programming, events or experiences. Nevertheless, what is important is the need to adopt an unbiased approach when attending to the care of others. At the same time there is a need to appreciate that this may be difficult for some care staff who might themselves have experienced sexual exploitation. Long-term unwanted memories certainly make it hard to attend to the care of a person whose behaviour is perceived to be sexually inappropriate. In the event of such circumstances, it would be best for the staff member as well as the person exhibiting the inappropriate behaviour to ask a supervisor for someone else to be assigned to that person's care. This makes for a much happier workplace for all concerned.

In concluding this chapter, it should be kept in mind that sexuality according to Hajjar *et al* (2004) "is a basic human need that begins at birth and continues throughout life". The purpose of describing all the component parts of sexuality in the concept of a rose, in this instance a rose that never wilts, is to emphasise that sexual desires and drives continue throughout the life cycle and for an older person are just as important as those of the young. The rose concept also helps the reader to understand that sexuality is much more than a physical act.

The unfurled rose petals show the many interconnecting intricacies which makes up human sexuality. People living with dementia may sometimes have gaps or difficulties in their ability to express their sexuality in appropriate ways; particularly in the areas of 'sensuality', 'intimacy' and 'identity'. Planning care and implementing individualised life-enhancing strategies to meet these deficits will be discussed in Part 3, 'Discovering Solutions'. It will also be shown throughout this book that sexuality, like a rose that never wilts, remains a constant in every person's adult life in one way or another.

CHAPTER TWO

Demystifying and Redefining Attitudes

This chapter will explore the origins of the negative social prejudices surrounding sexuality and people living with dementia. It will lay to rest a lot of myths and misconceptions that arise for care staff when faced with what is perceived as inappropriate sexual behaviour.

'What matters more than one's age, is maintaining a creative spirit that lasts a lifetime. You meet someone who is maybe in their 60s, 70s, even 80s and you meet them as that person, anyone beyond the age of retirement, so to speak. You seldom realise that they had a whole life of experience. They were just as virile and ingenious and capable as you believe yourself to be.'

Brad Pitt, Los Angeles Times (2009)

Sexuality is the thread of human existence and continues to flourish well into older age

Sexuality is a topic rarely discussed. This is not because of its unimportance but often due to care staff's discomfort with the subject. However, there are a lot of innuendos and giggles shared by care staff at the thought of a person living with dementia having an intimate sexual relationship. If a person living with dementia is seen to be pursuing any sexual drives or desires they are often looked upon with disdain. This negativity, like a ripple extending out on the water, can become widespread, and can be very damaging to the person. The person is often perceived and labelled as "a dirty old man" or "a dirty old woman" – a label that often sticks! Unfortunately negativity towards such sexual activities may be tied up with attitudes towards old age and disability generally.

Sexuality has long been regarded as an activity of younger people; especially those who are beautiful, tanned, slim, curvaceous, lithe and unwrinkled. This image is continually being reinforced by the advertisements in the media and trendy magazines. When these images are replaced with ones of older people being portrayed in a sexual light, keeping in mind that age might alter beauty but not spoil it (Kastenbaum, 1979), the image is nearly always portrayed with negativity. It is these negative images according to Minichiello *et al* (2005) that, "strongly shape societal beliefs about the older people and serve to reinforce the view that they are (or should be) sexually 'retired'". Therefore society, in general, commonly regards older and disabled people as asexual; people who couldn't possibly have any interest in sexual activities. As a consequence it is felt the subject of sexuality becomes increasingly insignificant the older a person becomes. These attitudes are supported by Ellis *et al*'s (2005) research that "the sexuality of older people remains largely stigmatised, stereotyped and shrouded in secrecy".

The secrecy is even worse if the person's sexual preference is to be homosexual. "Many lesbian and gay seniors," according to Birch (2009), "became adults at a time when homosexuality was considered to be unnatural, wrong, deviant and the basis for discrimination." Same sex partners in the past, Birch goes on to explain, "may have been accused of being sinners and forced to repent their evil ways. They may have been forced into therapy to cure their 'mental illness', which frequently included aversion therapies." Bygone memories, for this older generation, still linger on!

Dementia and Sexuality

As a consequence, most gay or lesbian older people, even in this day and age, still prefer to keep their own counsel regarding their homo-sexuality for fear of being labelled as deviant or discriminated against and their partner not being recognised as their principal carer.

To compound all the ongoing societal negative attitudes described above, ageism is rife in today's society. As a person's hair turns grey and they begin, perhaps, to appear physically frailer, their personhood is often undermined. They can be patronised or even belittled, status can be stripped away or they can be devalued and seen as unproductive old people, even if they are not! These views on ageing are commonly based on a person's chronological years (ageing appearance, grey hair for example), not their function.

> *A disturbing example of a patronising attitude was demonstrated when, one evening, 75-year-old, very active, grey haired Mrs Adams presented her membership card, as was the custom, to a receptionist for entry to the local gymnasium. Much to Mrs Adams's surprise and amusement the receptionist talked incessantly, thanking Mrs Adams for returning, for what was in the reception-ist's mind's eye, 'an obvious lost card'. Mrs Adams was unable to get a word in as the receptionist happily, but repeatedly, told Mrs Adams that "no stone would remain unturned until the card was returned to its rightful owner". She went on to say "if Mrs Adams liked to leave her phone number and address she was sure the rightful owner would like to thank her as well". To the embarrass-ment of the receptionist, fit Mrs Adams finally got a word in, replying, "Don't worry, dear, it is mine, and if you let me in I intend to go to the yoga class!"*

Perhaps the ageism and resultant prejudices also originate from a mistaken belief that sexual activity stops at 60 years of age, if not before. This stems from many young people's attitudes of not wanting to believe that their parents have a physical sexual relationship, thinking only that their parents' entire sexual activity was accounted for by the number of children in the family. Having such beliefs, it is certainly unlikely for a young person to contemplate, for example, sexual desires, drives and activity between their grandparents, especially if the grandparents are frail or either one of them has a diagnosis of dementia.

In the context of the sexual activity of older people, Bancroft (2009) observes: "the thread of human sexuality is densely woven into the fabric of human existence". Earlier research by Hajjar *et al* (2004) concluded that "human sexuality continues to flourish, whatever a person's age and it is just as important and fulfilling to older people as it is for the younger generation". Nay *et al* (2007) have also found that "for many older people being sexually active is important to their own sense of self and to their relationship".

Older people may have a different way of expressing themselves, especially in the intensity and frequency of sexual activity, but the need for close intimate relationships remains. Every older person has their own life history: a lifetime of memories, both happy and sorrowful which have certainly moulded their life's pathway. If they have had a fulfilling intimate relationship, either heterosexual or homosexual, then they will continue along this pathway as long as they do not have an overriding medical condition causing impotency or loss of libido. "Even in the face of life limiting illnesses", Lemieux *et al* (2004) found that "older people have reported that sexuality remains an important aspect of their lives even in the weeks or days prior to death".

Medical conditions that have an impact on the actual physical activity side of sexual functioning include stroke, cardiac problems, Parkinson's disease, diabetes, depression, dementia, rheumatoid arthritis and some types of surgery, for example radical prostatectomy for prostate cancer. Some forms of surgery can also have an impact as well on how a person views their self-image or sensual appeal, especially following a mastectomy or colostomy. Helping the person to understand and adjust to the changes is important because a lot can be done to help maintain sexual expression for older people experiencing these conditions.

Reviewing medication, taking pain relief before the sexual act, supporting limbs and adjusting positions, choosing the time of day when a person is not tired, finding alternative erogenous zones, wearing an

Dementia and Sexuality

attractive cummerbund to cover a colostomy bag, applying vaginal lubrication, and using appropriate sex aids are just a few strategies that can help maintain physical sexual functioning. Some people may need to seek advice from a sex therapist. Kuhn (2002) has documented that "when older people are not involved in an intimate or sexually active relationship, it is primarily due to lack of an available partner".

The loss of a partner can bring untold grief as well as the loss of an ongoing physical relationship. As a consequence the person may seek comfort from another intimate relationship which, depending on circumstances, could be provided by a new partner of the same or opposite sex.

Changing sexual orientation might create opposition from family members. However it also needs to be appreciated that, just like heterosexual couples, same sex residents, according to Kuhn (2002) "who become couples may simply enjoy conversing and participating in activities together. Friendship may be all that is needed and sought". In these circumstances family members and care staff need to keep an open mind.

The onset of dementia can create challenges for both the primary carer and paid care staff. Embarrassment and frustration can run high for primary family carers, and care staff often find it difficult to broach the topic. However, an integral part of the problem solving process is to approach and discuss the issue in an open and flexible manner, gathering information about the person's life story and sexual past with empathy and respect.

Care staff need to be aware that people living with dementia can openly express their sexual desires in many different ways. Such behaviour can include suggestive language or gestures, fondling or exposing themselves, making unwanted sexual advances or stripping off clothing, as well as seeking sexual encounters from someone who is not their spouse. Sometimes if the person is having an overriding delusional experience, spouses are accused of having an affair with the care staff. These actions are often an indication of unmet sexual needs but certainly can be very offensive to both spouse and care staff alike.

Case study – Mr Borelli
Recent deterioration in daily living functions.
74 years old, Mr Borelli was admitted to a low dependency residential care facility following the recent death of his wife. His family felt he could no longer live alone.

Presenting problem
Mr Borelli was seeking a sexual relationship with a co-resident who had dementia. Care staff disapproved of the liaison.

Staff documented, a few weeks after Mr Borelli's admission, that he had become quite attached to Mrs Clarke, a co-resident. Care staff were anxious to separate the two because Mrs Clarke had a diagnosis of Alzheimer's disease and it was thought that Mr Borelli might take sexual advantage of her. Staff felt that although Mr Borelli was demonstrating some cognitive impairment, he should know his liaison with Mrs Clarke was inappropriate, especially since his own wife had just died. The couple were continually being separated and constantly reprimanded. Mr Borelli was labelled 'a lecherous old man'.

On obtaining a sexual history from Mr Borelli it was found that he and his wife had a long-term, loving and intimate relationship. Mr Borelli stated with a great deal of emotion "it was my very being and my wife's too!". It was noted, during the problem solving process, that Mr Borelli had been the prime carer for his wife right up until the day she died.

After a few weeks of carefully observing Mr Borelli's interaction with Mrs Clarke, the care staff came to realise that instead of Mr Borelli being 'lecherous' he was actually transferring his on-going caring role to help and offer companionship to the lonely, frail, cognitively impaired Mrs Clarke. Mr Borelli was helping Mrs Clarke to feel more secure and valued, in what appeared to her to be a new and strange environment. In actual fact Mr Borelli was Mrs Clarke's benefactor not her predator!

The families of both residents were informed and at first they were quite concerned. However, after ongoing discussions and reassurance that Mrs Clarke was not being coerced into the relationship, both families came to accept the situation. A good outcome resulted as Mr Borelli's interpersonal interaction with Mrs Clarke became an integral part of her care.

Dementia and Sexuality

If any overt sexual behaviour occurs in a residential aged care setting, the care staff can become frustrated with the situation, particularly if they have little time, knowledge or the skills to react appropriately and deal with such behaviour constructively.

Lack of understanding or overreaction by care staff can lead to chastising, excluding the person from 'in-home' social gatherings, requesting sedation be prescribed or even chemical castration. This of course does little to identify, or solve the problem of, the person's unmet sexual needs.

Before any problem solving can begin, care staff need to examine their own attitudes, prejudices or experiences, which may have a marked effect on addressing what are, at times, complex and challenging issues. In

Case study – Mr Jarrard
Frontotemporal lobe dysfunction.
54 years old, Mr Jarrard was diagnosed with younger onset dementia five years before moving into a residential care setting.
Presenting problem
Communication breakdown with the 'person responsible' – Mr Doyle.

Mr Jarrard's family had long disassociated themselves from the homosexual couple, except for Mr Jarrard's sister who remained in touch. Although Mr Doyle had a high-powered business role, he had been able, with the help of community services and a little input from the sister, to juggle his working role with his carer's role until six months ago. It was in this period of time that Mr Jarrard became more and more dependent for all his daily living activities. After a meeting with the service providers it was decided that residential care was advisable to provide the full time care that Mr Jarrard required.

Mr Doyle visited his partner every evening, but soon found that the care staff were seeking information, including life history, from Mr Jarrard's sister. Mr Doyle tried to set the records straight saying he was the primary carer, 'the person responsible', but to no avail. The care staff had formed their own opinion that the sister certain instances it may be necessary for some members of the care staff to seek professional counselling in order to work through any personal traumatic sexual exploitation experiences they may have encountered, as discussed in the previous chapter. Approaching the problems without any pre-existing biases is important so that negative views do not override the quality of care provided to the individual person.

An example of care staff bias can be demonstrated by the case study of Mr Borelli on page 29.

In another case study (below) taking time to know the person living with dementia's sexual orientation on his admission to a residential care facility might have prevented a lot of distress for his primary same sex carer. The two men had been partners for almost 27 years.

was the blood relation and therefore had to be the next of kin. They did not appreciate the significance of Mr Doyle's responsible person role.

After all his years of caring for Mr Jarrard, taking responsibility, the close relationship they had shared together, Mr Doyle now felt invisible because the valuable lifestyle information he continually offered the care staff was ignored. He felt devastated when he heard snide remarks from the care staff about his relationship with Mr Jarrard.

Of course there were days when Mr Jarrard did not know who he was, so how could he convey to the staff the intimate relationship he and Mr Jarrard had once shared, and the loss, grief and emotional let-down he was now experiencing. A lot of background data could have been gathered if the care staff, as Manthorpe (2003) suggests, were to "recognise the importance of partners and also friends as alternative family networks".

It is important that care staff realise that a 'person responsible' for health and well being is not necessarily the next of kin. The 'person responsible' can be the most recent spouse or de facto spouse with whom the person has a close, continuing relationship. 'De facto spouse' includes same sex partners (Guardianship Tribunal, N.S.W. 2009).

Dementia and Sexuality

As shown by the two different case studies the negative attitudes and biases, especially Mr Doyle's 'invisibility' and grief, could have been eliminated if both life and sexual histories including sexual preferences had been taken and discussed on admission to the residential care facility. Ideally, this type of information needs to become part of any residential care facility's admission protocol and the resident's specific needs should be incorporated in the person-centred care planning.

Unfortunately, however, an older or same sex person's sexual relationships, with or without the added diagnosis of dementia, are seldom talked about, either with the individual person or as part of the agenda of a staff case conference. This is not because it is an unimportant topic but because the care staff feel ill at ease with the subject.

Care staff need to seek out and take every possible opportunity offered to discuss ways of breaking down attitudinal barriers. It is through education that knowledge and awareness of each individual's unmet sexual needs will increase, negativity will be overcome and all the old myths, misconceptions and social prejudices will be laid to rest. McAuliffe *et al* (2007) confirm this need, documenting "it is the responsibility of every health professional who works with older people to help replace societal myths regarding sexuality and ageing with positive images that celebrate the sexuality of older people and normalize this important part of living".

CHAPTER THREE

Exploring How Dementia Can Impact on Sexuality

The aim of this chapter is to examine the brain's role in the human sexual response cycle. By understanding what happens in the healthy brain we are in a better position to understand disruptions to the process. With understanding, comes the ability to develop effective management strategies.

*'Nothing in life is to be feared, it is only to be understood.
Now is the time to understand more,
so that we may fear less'*

Marie Curie

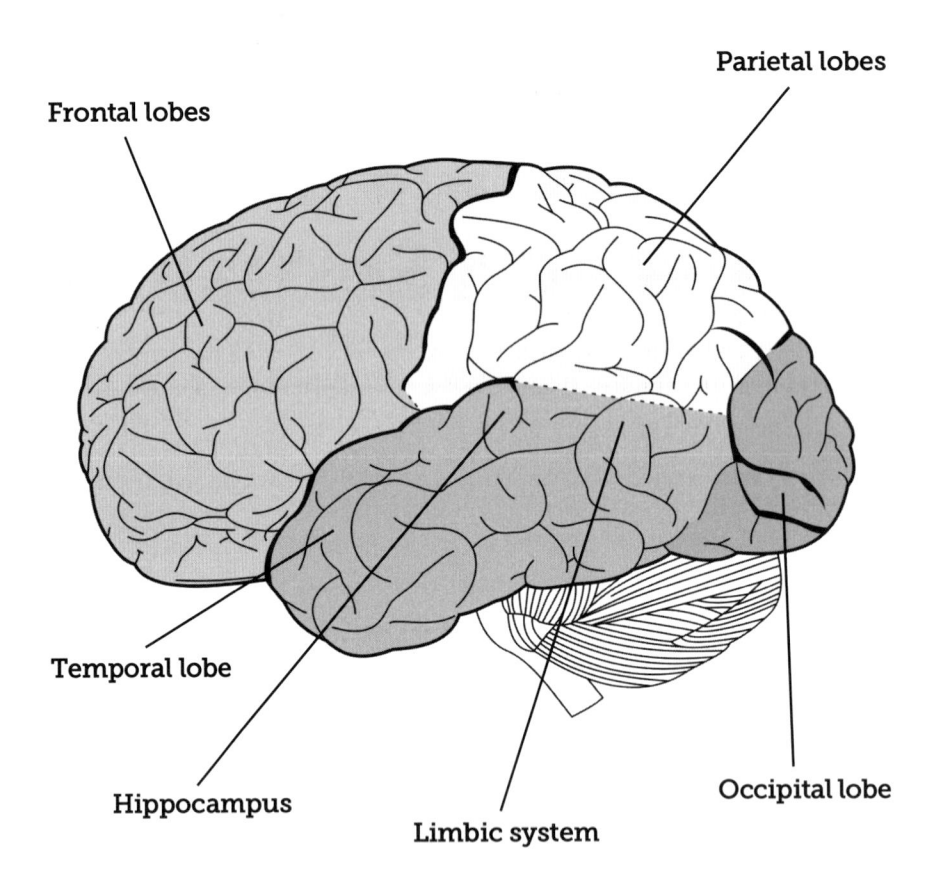

Parietal lobes

Frontal lobes

Temporal lobe

Hippocampus

Limbic system

Occipital lobe

The lobes of the brain shown from the left-hand side

Exploring How Dementia Can Impact on Sexuality

All human behaviour is mediated by brain activity. From the blinking of an eye, to our awareness of our own existence, the brain is involved in "movement, perception, language, behaviour, emotion, thought and memory" (Bancroft, 2009). All this is made possible by the interlinking of the separate areas of the brain, each with specific functions. It is no surprise then that a person living with dementia can display a wide range of unusual and at times inappropriate behaviour. This is perhaps no more aptly portrayed than in the realm of human sexuality.

Many areas of the brain are involved in the human sexual response. When some or many of these areas are affected by dementia, it is not uncommon to observe very inappropriate sexual behaviour. This can cause much distress to all those involved in the care of the person. Nevertheless, people living with dementia continue to need the same close relationships as any other person, though there will be apparent differences in their ability to give and receive love and affection, depending on the type of dementia each person has. This in turn influences how they will express their sexuality. The common types of dementia and their symptoms include:

- Alzheimer's disease: Memory loss, vagueness, word finding and conversation difficulties, routine tasks take longer, deterioration in social skills, emotional unpredictability
- Vascular dementia: Patchy memory, mood swings, lability, difficulty with speech and language
- Dementia with Lewy bodies: Difficulties with concentration, attention and judging distances. Extreme confusion, visual hallucinations, delusions, depression, tremors and stiffness
- Frontotemporal dementia: Changes in character, social behaviour and language, obsessive and repetitive actions and phrases, word finding difficulties
- Alcohol related dementia: Decreased alertness and attentiveness, inability to grasp all elements of the immediate situation, inability to make decisions. Loss of inhibition.

Dementia and Sexuality

The human brain could be described as the body's computer. Like a computer system the brain has many compartments that receive, analyse, sort, store, file, memorise, link and programme information that can be processed into all aspects of daily function. Functions include the ability to think, plan actions appropriately, recognise familiar people, objects and surroundings, follow directions or instructions, respond emotionally, control behaviour or attend to business/financial affairs.

If a computer was to fail (due perhaps to an electricity power cut, flat batteries or virus contamination) the whole system could break down and all the stored information and functions could be disrupted or even lost. The same change can be seen when the function of the human brain has been damaged by the process of dementia, especially in the complex area of expressing a person's sexual needs and desires. For example, what was previously attended to in private (fondling themselves, disrobing, or at times making inappropriate gestures or advances to others) may now be done in the open, with no awareness of the surrounding environment.

In order to explore the impact dementia has on the area of sexual expression, it is useful to review the brain's anatomical structure.

Brain structure (see page 34)

It is well documented that the brain has two cerebral hemispheres. The left side is described as the dominant side and controls the right side of the body. Conversely, the right side of the brain is usually the non dominant side, and controls the left side of the body. The hemispheres are divided into four lobes, frontal, temporal, parietal and occipital, and deep within the brain is the limbic system, a group of structures which initiates sexual emotions among other functions.

Each area of the brain, broadly speaking, has a different function. There are also numerous neuronal pathways linking these structures. If any of these lobes or structures are affected by the process of dementia, dysfunction or changes in behaviour may become evident.

Limbic system

The limbic system is described as "a set of evolutionarily primitive brain structures deep within the brain" (Bailey, 2010). Included in this group are the hippocampus, hypothalamus, amygdala, thalamus, pituitary gland and several other structures whose functions include storing and processing our closely connected emotions and long term memories. (Medline Plus, 2009).

The limbic system controls the autonomic and endocrine function, our awake/sleep cycle, our motivations and mood. The amygdala and hypothalamus, in particular play a large part in the emotional aspects of our lives including fear and anxiety as well as sexual desire, arousal and orgasm (Bailey, 2010).

The frontal lobes

Creasey (2004) describes the frontal lobes "as the executive centre of the brain, the manager, decision maker". There are three basic parts:

- Lateral - Planning, organising, learning, reasoning, personality, insight
- Medial - Initiation (the starter motor)
- Orbito-basal – Regulation of behaviour including socially appropriate behaviour and social and moral judgment. It works by receiving feedback and responding appropriately (Creasey, 2004).

In addition, the frontal lobes contain the brain areas that control movements.

The temporal lobes

The temporal lobes have an important role in storing memory, both verbal and visual. To summarise Lezak's (1995) description: the left side of the brain, usually the dominant side, controls verbal function; words and names. The non-dominant right side of the brain controls visual function, including high level functioning in perception and recognition, for example recognising faces and scenes.

Dementia and Sexuality

As well as memory, both sides of the temporal lobes process:

- hearing
- smell and taste
- language reception and understanding
- musical awareness.

The hippocampus is one of the groups of structures within the limbic system, and is embedded in the temporal lobe. It is a critical structure in memory 'circuits', saving and retrieving long term memories. It also ties together visual memories with sounds and smells and fixes them in space and time (Boeree, 2010). It is a part of the brain which often shows the first changes in Alzheimer's disease and these changes can be detected in brain scans.

The parietal lobes
According to Creasey (2004) the parietal lobes have the following functions:

- "Dominant side – Analytical and logic centre, responsible for things that have structure; language, speech, writing, reading, calculation and sequencing skills; appreciation of the position of body parts and things that come in order
- Non-dominant – Geography, where we are in the world, space appreciation of self, others and objects and direction or navigation around the environment. It also differentiates between, up, down; side, front and behind
- The parietal lobes take the words stored in the temporal lobe and put the words into action."

Johnson (2009) states that "the parietal lobe also controls sensation, touch, pressure as well as fine perception of sensation; judgment of texture, weight, size, shape etc."

Two other functions stemming from the parietal lobe according to Creasey (2004) are:

- "Praxis – ability to carry out previously learned purposeful movements or patterns of movement, important in daily living skills, dressing, bathing
- Gnosis – ability to recognise things for what they are; facial images, objects or surroundings."

Case study – Mr Sanderson

Loss of inhibition.

73 years old, Mr Sanderson was diagnosed with Alzheimer's disease, and recently moved into a low care residential setting.

Presenting problem

Mr Sanderson was continually masturbating in public as well as trying to pull care staff into bed with him.

Care staff were finding Mr Sanderson's overt behaviour and his unwanted sexual advances very offensive. This behaviour had previously surfaced at home and was one reason why his primary carer, Mrs Sanderson, had looked for placement in the residential facility.

It seemed likely that damage to Mr Sanderson's frontal lobe had caused the anti-social behaviour. Bancroft (2009) explains: "It is through the cognitive processes of the frontal lobe that the whole gamut of social and interpersonal influences impinges upon our sexuality." However, when a person has dementia any one of these interconnecting pathways may become damaged or disrupted, resulting in changes in sexual responses and behaviour.

In broad terms, the frontal lobe is the keeper of our code of conduct, our customs, moral standards and proprieties and if damaged by the process of dementia, rules and regulations and personal standards can become eroded.

Therefore it is easy to see why Mr Sanderson was no longer responsible for his actions. He no longer had insight or awareness. His social graces and boundaries were forgotten; he now acted on impulse following his needs, stemming from the limbic system, because his powers of inhibition to control impulsive or inappropriate behaviour, be it sexual or social, had become diminished.

Dementia and Sexuality

Case Study - Mr Darcy

Temporal lobe impairment.
70 years old, with a diagnosis of Alzheimer's disease, Mr Darcy lived in a dementia-specific residential unit.

Presenting problem

Mr Darcy was continually misinterpreting verbal instructions from his wife.

Mrs Darcy, who made daily visits, saw a tired husband, and told him "it is time for bed, dear". Unfortunately, Mr Darcy, now lacking in comprehension, misconstrued the meaning of the instruction and in his mind associated past bedtime experiences with 'time for physical sexual activity'. He eagerly pulled Mrs Darcy to his bed but she, embarrassed by her husband's action within the care setting, rejected him, leaving him bewildered and more confused than ever. Unfortunately Mr Darcy did not have the ability to understand that the time and place, on this occasion, was not appropriate or pleasurable for his wife.

Mr Darcy's misinterpretation can be easily explained if there is an appreciation that the temporal lobe is involved in saving and retrieving long term memories. Arnell (1997) states "it is the first part of the brain to be damaged by Alzheimer's disease; memory loss and disorientation appear among the first symptoms". Short term memory is lost first. The words "it is time for bed, dear" triggered Mr Darcy's past and, what were obviously for him, pleasurable memories, encouraging him to engage his wife in sexual activity.

In addition Griffith *et al* (1993) explain: "There can also be profound communication loss that is associated with temporal lobe dysfunction; not appreciating the delicate signals that a person is or is not ready for sexual activity. Also the loss of ability to understand what is or is not mutually pleasurable about any sexual activity." Another issue associated with temporal lobe dysfunction that might raise problems for a spouse or partner is when a person insists on repetitive sexual activity, having already forgotten the act was just completed.

The occipital lobes

The smallest lobe of the brain, explained by Griffiths *et al* (1993) "as the vision and visual perception centre, responsible for:

- Visual memory — receives and interprets raw sensory information from the outside world
- Recognition of visual symbols, shapes and colours
- Reading."

The sexual response cycle

The initial sensations of the human sexual response cycle, described by Masters and Johnson (1966) as "sexual desire, arousal and orgasm", are initiated within structures of the limbic system. Interaction with the frontal lobe and the visceral autonomic body motor responses are also needed. The frontal lobe, according to Bancroft (2009), "processes the sexual meaning of what is happening; external events and internal imagery and fantasy". It responds to the sexual urges within the limbic system, initiating judgment and action or moderating the urges if necessary.

The visceral automatic body responses, summarising Bancroft (2009), react to sexual arousal and excitement by increasing the heart and breathing rate, making the necessary vascular changes — erection of penis or clitoris — and stimulates vaginal lubrication and associated reactions such as breast engorgement and skin flush. Bancroft (2009) adds, "a heightened awareness of pleasurable erotic sensations climaxes with orgasm" followed by "resolution: returning the sex organs to the prearousal state" (Griffith *et al*, 1993).

The temporal and other lobes are involved in the sexual response as well. Memories and visual contextual clues all play their role in the sexual response cycle.

Disruptions to the sexual function

Some challenging behaviours, together with an explanation of the area of the brain that is predominantly involved, are described below. It should be emphasised, though, that whilst each area of the brain has its own function, each should not be viewed in isolation but as part of a complex, interconnected structure.

Dementia and Sexuality

Problems arise in the limbic system when the process of dementia accentuates the person's libido or disrupts the connecting pathways of long term memories (stored in the hippocampus) and emotions. As these emotions are tied in with a frontal lobe that may be damaged as well, aggressive emotional outbursts may occur when a person is prevented or cautioned about any inappropriate sexual behaviour.

Another problem originating within the limbic group of structures is the disruption to the 'sleep-wake cycle' controlled by the hypothalamus and suprachiasmatic nucleus. This problem accompanies dementia with Lewy bodies. The loss of the normal day-night cycle leads to fragmented and disrupted patterns of sleep. Disrupted sleep may also

Case study: Mr Jones
Frontotemporal lobe impairment.
52 years old, Mr Jones was diagnosed with younger onset dementia, and lived in a high-level residential care unit.
Presenting problem
Mr Jones was continually exposing himself and masturbating in public.

Mr Jones used obscene language and continually made inappropriate and unwanted sexual advances to care staff. He had no insight that his behaviour was unacceptable and therefore there was no reasoning with him, and if reprimanded for his actions he would become very emotionally abusive.

Mr Jones was diagnosed with younger onset dementia when his brain imaging showed he had a combination of frontal and temporal lobe dysfunction. Younger onset dementia usually begins between 40 and 65 years of age. "There are no true memory losses as seen in Alzheimer's disease but there are marked changes in personality. There are gradual changes in the customary ways of behaving and responding emotionally to others; loss of social inhibitory skills and bad language." (Feinberg School of Medicine, 2009) This diagnosis did explain why Mr Jones unabashedly exposed himself, masturbated in public, and used such uncouth language as well as his continual unwanted sexual suggestions and advances.

be a result of spouse/partner separation making the person uneasy, looking for their partner.

It seems that the major behavioural changes that affect the frontal lobes occur when there is some form of Alzheimer's disease, vascular dementia, dementia with Lewy bodies or frontotemporal dementia, resulting in loss of social inhibition and the accompanying inappropriate sexual behaviour.

The case study on page 39 demonstrates frontal lobe dysfunction.

Case study: Mr Field
Occipital lobe impairment.
76 years old, Mr Field, diagnosed with vascular dementia, lived in a residential care facility.
Presenting problem
Mr Field was continually trying to fondle care staff whilst they were attending to his personal hygiene. When the opportunity arose he would try and pull the staff into his bed.

On assessing Mr Field it was found that he was only attracted to some of the health staff; there were really only five young ladies involved. The common denominator was that they all had blue eyes and blonde hair. Whilst interviewing Mr Field's daughter it was discovered that his wife, who had recently died, did have the same colouring of blue eyes and blonde hair. This fact did explain a lot.

As a result of the vascular dementia, Mr Field was living in his past memory and was, 'in his mind's eye', interacting with his wife. He shows the involvement and overlapping of both the parietal and the occipital lobes. The occipital lobe, as previously stated by Griffiths *et al* (1993), "is the vision and visual perception centre". The obvious agnosia problems he was experiencing, an inability to recognise familiar things for what they were (facial image misidentification), stemmed from the parietal lobe. However, the visual memory was still intact within the occipital lobe, which explained why Mr Field mistook a staff member for his spouse.

Dementia and Sexuality

Case study: Mr Evans
Parietal lobe impairment.
Mr Evans, 72, was diagnosed with vascular dementia and living in a dementia-specific residential unit.
Presenting problem
Mr Evans did not recognise his own strength, and in the past had injured his spouse. He also used to disrobe and wander into adjacent bedrooms causing concern to co-residents.

Each time Mrs Evans visited her large and still sturdy husband, he repeatedly and vigorously hugged her frail body in an endeavour to show his affection. He also tightly squeezed Mrs Evans' arthritic hands and in both instances caused her a great deal of pain. Despite her explanations and protests Mr Evans did not understand that his actions were causing her physical harm. As a result Mrs Evans tried to avoid close contact, much to the irritation and agitation of her husband.

Dysfunction to the dominant parietal lobe results in a great many problems as was evident by Mr Evans' actions. The person may not be able to concentrate on what another person is saying or even logically analyse what is being said. Certainly they do not

There can be other complications within the occipital lobe. Hallucinations are common in people with dementia, especially dementia due to Lewy bodies – for example, seeing a naked person.

Care staff need to be aware that these visual experiences may lead to possible inappropriate sexual arousal and excitement. Validation therapy, following a sexual history, can be a useful strategy in these situations and will be discussed later.

In summary, the evidence is that the person living with dementia is not deliberately behaving inappropriately. They are not dirty old men or women nor are they 'sexually deviant'. Their behaviour is out of their control because of damage or disruption to one or several lobes of their brain or the interrelated structures within the limbic system. In order to bring comfort and well being to the person living with dementia, a know why they do things nor do they appreciate the subtleties of what is being said. They may also perseverate, repeating the same remarks or actions previously made, over and over again.

Mr Evans' parietal dysfunction had altered his comprehension such that his actions were not acceptable. Similarly he was not able to understand the 'hands-up, back off' gestures from Mrs Evans, indicating his actions were inappropriate and unacceptable. As a result of dysfunction of this type, Mr Evans was not aware of his own strength.

Mr Evans' vascular dementia may also have caused some spatial impairment (non-dominant parietal lobe dysfunction), resulting in a loss of awareness of directions or surrounding environment, and this could explain disrobing, wandering and getting into the wrong beds. The disrobing could also stem from apraxia, an inability to carry out previously learned patterns of dressing, having taken his clothing off to get ready for bed but then not knowing the sequence to put his night attire on. As a result of this impairment, Mr Evans was wrongly suspected of being sexually 'deviant' and trying to get into bed with a person who was not his spouse. In actual fact he was simply preparing for bed.

thorough assessment is needed by the care staff to discover what areas of the brain are damaged. Goals can be set accordingly, and care planned and implemented that will fill the gaps in the person's unmet sexual needs.

PART TWO

Sustaining Relationships

'I believe that one of the most important things to learn in life is that you can make a difference in your community no matter who you are or where you live.
I have seen so many good deeds, people helped, lives improved, because someone cared...
Do what you can to show you care about other people, and you will make our world a better place'

Rosalynn Carter

CHAPTER FOUR

Engaging with Primary Carers

This chapter addresses the complexities faced by the primary carer in the home setting. The primary carer may be a spouse, partner, or significant other such as a family member or neighbour or friend who attends to the day-to-day functions of the person living with dementia.

'To the world you may be just one person, but to one person you may be the world'

Josephine Billings

Dementia and Sexuality

People have been living with their dementia long before the diagnosis is made. Primary carers are usually the first to notice the changes. They may report vagueness, forgetfulness or misplacing things and when the person is challenged by the carer, they may make excuses that it is "just old age" or "I think I am entitled to forget things at my age".

However when a diagnosis of dementia is made, it is a very emotional time for both the person living with dementia and the primary carer. Whilst 'dementia' might be just a word to some, for many it still has an associated stigma, connotations of mental illness or senility that can have an overwhelming effect on the person and their carer.

At the same time, for some people, the diagnosis of dementia can be a relief. People have been known to say, "thank goodness I only have dementia, I thought I had Alzheimer's disease". Most people have no understanding that the word 'dementia' is used "to describe the symptoms of a large number of illnesses that cause a progressive decline in brain function. It is a broad term which describes a loss of memory, intellect, rationality, social skills and normal emotional reactions." (Alzheimer's Australia, 2005).

Dementia is caused by one or a combination of diseases that affect the brain. The most common diseases are:

- Alzheimer's disease
- Vascular dementia
- Dementia with Lewy bodies
- Frontotemporal dementia
- Alcohol related dementia.

"When one's marital partner receives a diagnosis of dementia," Harris (2009) explains, "it has major reverberating ramifications for a couple. Such a diagnosis affects every aspect of their marital lives, including the most intimate areas, for the well partner often moves from being a lover to becoming a caregiver, taking on more and more of the responsibility for her or his ill partner's daily care." There can be a lot of understandable grief and loss to work through – grief for the ongoing illness, its impact and the loss of the future they had planned together.

Unfortunately dementia is an ongoing illness. The loss of memory initially causes difficulty in performing familiar tasks. The primary carer usually fills in the gaps readily, offering small amounts of help at first with eating, dressing, bathing and toileting. Gradually the amount of care needed increases as the person's judgment and ability to make decisions decreases over time, often without the primary carer realising it.

The person living with dementia often gets confused about time and place, even becoming disorientated in familiar surroundings. Actions and speech can become repetitive and simple 'word finding' can be difficult; the person can't communicate what they are thinking and so they are unable to make their needs known. A lot of frustrations may build up for both the person living with dementia and their primary carer. What started out as a helping, prompting or guiding role for the primary carer can progress into a full-time caring role, day and night, seven days a week.

Keeping connected is very important; the primary carer does have to exercise a lot of patience, hard as it may be at times. Humour often helps, laughing with the person living with dementia, not at them. Accepting that the changes in personality and function are a result of the process of dementia is also a positive thing to do. If a couple have had a close intimate relationship prior to the dementia then maintaining this relationship according to Harris (2009) can be "a major contributor in their quality of life. Indeed, when memory is gone, it is this intimacy that may provide an important bridge to the past".

There may be alterations in the way the intimacy is expressed, so there may need to be some negotiation. For example the 'affective level of intimacy', described by Moss *et al* (1993) and the emotional depth and closeness a couple share, may provide comforting gratification for both parties: hugging, kissing, cuddling and being physically close. Physical intercourse may no longer be sustainable or required in the later stages of dementia. Sherman (1998) explains: "When new patterns of intimacy can be established early in the course of dementia, they appear to be maintained for some time in the later stages."

Whilst the primary carer continues to give the best possible care, they can become emotionally and physically drained. This is when help is

Dementia and Sexuality

needed from community services. These can share the day-to-day load of caring with the primary carer, allowing them some time to catch up on any outstanding family or personal issues as well as to take time out in order to adjust to their caring role and do the things necessary to maintain their own health and well-being. Attending a carer support group may also be invaluable help to the primary carer as well as giving them an opportunity to increase their knowledge and skills about dementia, and to share with other carers the impact dementia has on their world.

Most carers will say that they have had no formal training on becoming a carer! Burns (2010) agrees: "A carer is a person who happens into the position by chance. As a consequence a carer needs time to adjust and to open up and not be afraid to ask the questions that need to be asked, so they can get the answers they need to make the caring role much easier." A lot of these questions, especially on issues concerning sexual expression, and their answers can be discussed in carer support group meetings to the benefit of all present. By attending a support group carers have an opportunity to network, and share their feelings and experiences.

Keep in mind that programmes such as Living with Memory Loss can be of benefit. "These groups are specifically designed for people in the early stage of dementia and people with memory loss can go alone if they wish. In each programme the opportunity to separate and discuss relevant issues is provided for people living with memory loss and their family member or friend. Ongoing support is provided after the conclusion of the programme." (Alzheimer's Australia, 2008).

It might not be so easy for someone in a same-sex relationship to attend and open up to a mixed group of carers. They may have hidden their relationship in order to meet society's expectations of people of the same sex living together, hiding under an 'umbrella' as friends sharing a home for financial or similar reasons. Nevertheless to fully gain information, participate and share feelings within a support group, Mackenzie (2009) states "the person will have to 'come out'". Mackenzie further explains, "coming out frequently carries some foreboding, typically it is exhausting and this is exacerbated when the person coming out feels vulnerable". It is wise therefore that the same sex partner makes contact with the group's facilitator so the facilitator knows in advance of the meeting the sexual orientation of a new member. Vulnerability hopefully will vanish when the gay or lesbian person is reassured that policies and procedures of carer support groups are to facilitate an environment for open, comfortable discussion, and the philosophy includes the principle that "whatever information or feelings are shared at the meeting, nothing ever is to leave the room" (Mackenzie, 2009).

It is when the primary carer finds that the ongoing progression of dementia leads to marked changes in behaviour, such as disturbed sleep patterns, wandering, aggression, urinary and faecal incontinence, and especially inappropriate sexual behaviour due to the loss of inhibitions, that the situation becomes difficult to manage. However, there are many ways to overcome these challenges, as the case studies in this chapter demonstrate.

Nocturia and incontinence

Disturbed sleep may stem from nocturia, a complaint whereby the individual has to wake at night one or more times to empty their bladder (Van Kerrebroeck *et al*, 2002.) Once up, the person is often unable to find their way back to their bed. They wander around their house and, becoming distressed, anxiety sets in and they become wide awake. Meanwhile the carer, now wide awake themselves, guides the person back to bed. Both the person and the carer have difficulty getting back to sleep, as Mr Delaney's case study demonstrates (page 54). A night light can help solve the disorientation problem. A commode beside the bed can also help women. Similarly a urinal or a bucket at close reach for men can aid urination with less sleep disturbance. It can be helpful if the primary carer uses some iridescent paint to mark the rim of the bucket. This makes the bucket very visible at night.

Urinary incontinence is another problem that can be associated with growing older. This is not always the case and is certainly not an inevitable accompaniment of dementia. The person can have any one of the problems that a cognitive functioning person may have. Instead of just using absorbent pads, a visit to a continence advisory service will initiate the problem-solving process.

Dementia and Sexuality

Case study: Mr Delaney
Frontal lobe impairment.
71 years old, Mr Delaney was diagnosed with Alzheimer's disease 18 months ago, living at home in the care of his wife.
Presenting problem
Nocturia.

Nocturia woke Mr Delaney on a regular basis. When he got up to empty his bladder, he could not get off to sleep again. Unfortunately for Mrs Delaney, her presence lying beside him sexually aroused him and night after night Mr Delaney made ardent sexual demands on his physically tired wife. He seemed to forget all the pleasurable foreplay that both partners used to enjoy. The rough handling and repetitive sexual intimate requests, Mr Delaney having forgotten the previous encounter, formed a difficult situation for the sleep-deprived Mrs Delaney to cope with. It is easy to realise how this sort of constant behaviour could put a strain on what was once a loving relationship. Mrs Delaney told the community care staff that "it is hard to be a lover when you wipe your husband's bottom, especially when he has forgotten all the loving gentle encounters we once shared".

Nocturia is often a problem as a person grows older. It is not just related to dementia – there can be many causes and the condition needs thorough investigation. Help can be available from a continence advisory service, usually situated within an acute hospital or a community health centre. In Mr Delaney's case his problem was related to an enlarged prostate and he was referred to a urologist for treatment. Once the nocturia was rectified Mr Delaney slept through the night and did not disturb his wife, much to her relief.

Sometimes when absorbent pads are used and it is time to change the pad, inappropriate sexual arousal can result, especially from a man living with dementia. The unexpected sexual arousal may take the primary carer or the visiting community care staff who are preparing him for a shower by surprise. There can be a shock reaction from the community staff member in attendance, and of course a lot of embarrassment and distress to the primary carer. The primary carer is usually a wife who fervently apologises for the inappropriate behaviour. However, the unwanted and unexpected sexual advances or remarks made at this time can be explained quite simply. A female attending to a task encompassing a male's genitalia can trigger sexual arousal and, in the case of the male with dysfunctional cognitive ability, he is unable to appreciate the reality or the meaning of what is happening. Hence the behaviour!

The primary carer needs to know that these situations can be avoided if the person living with dementia's urinary incontinence is meticulously assessed. The type of incontinence can be identified and appropriate treatment implemented. A successful continence programme may be possible which avoids the use of absorbent pads and the trigger to the sexual arousal is thus removed.

The aggressive behaviour that primary carers find difficult to work with can also stem from constipation. Constipation can trigger aggression, although the connection of the two conditions is rarely thought about. As a person ages their muscles lose some of their ability to contract. This has a big bearing on the muscle within the bowel. This muscle is a bit like a caterpillar, rising back on itself and pushing forward. This action moves the faecal waste forward along the gastrointestinal tract, ready to be evacuated when convenient.

The ageing process slows the progress of the forward faecal movement often resulting in faecal matter becoming impacted high in the colon in the large intestine. This impaction causes a lot of discomfort and pain and the person can become agitated. If the condition is ignored the agitation can eventually develop into a highly aggressive state.

Faecal impaction can also cause faecal incontinence. Our amazing body mechanisms do try to compensate for any irregularities. In the case of faecal impaction, the body produces fluid that acts to lubricate the faecal hard matter so it can be moved along the bowel. This fluid picks up the colour stain from the faeces and eventually seeps past the anus to the outside surface; it is often mistaken for diarrhoea. Absorbent pads may be used to contain this faecal incontinence, and the fitting or removal of them becomes another trigger for unwanted sexual arousal. The solution is to prevent constipation, and both the source of aggression and sexual inappropriateness will be eliminated.

A good regime to prevent constipation, adapted from Briggs (2004), is to:

- Have a drink of hot water half an hour prior to breakfast
- Establish a regular time for bowel evacuation preferably half an hour after breakfast
- Increase fluids gradually, 8 – 10 cups daily, as long as the person does not have a cardiac or kidney problem
- Exercise regularly, walking 20 minutes per day slightly puffing
- Eat a good high fibre diet; wholegrain bread, three fruits and five vegetables daily.

Case study: Mrs Owens
Emotional unpredictability and deterioration in social skills.
77 years old, Mrs Owens was diagnosed with Alzheimer's disease two years previously, being cared for by her husband in their own home.
Presenting problem
Jealousy and paranoia.

Mrs Owens received daily visits from community care staff who attended to showering and other hygiene needs. Unfortunately, much to the embarrassment of Mr Owens and the current young female care staff, Mrs Owens repeatedly accused them both of having an affair behind her back. She became quite paranoid in her thinking, repeatedly saying "I hear what you say, all the giggles and laughter, I know what you are up to, sex together when my back is turned".

No rational discussion could persuade Mrs Owens to think differently. Other members of the care staff team were tried and the accusations stopped when male staff attended. However, it was not always possible for the service to roster male assistants and whenever a young female assistant attended the jealousy continued. Mr Owens felt his wife's jealousy was a huge problem and, whilst he needed the help, he felt ill-prepared to deal with the consequences.

Jealousy was not new for the couple. Mrs Owens had never let her husband out of her sight when attending social events. Mr

Pressures on the primary carer

There are a lot of pressures put on the primary carer, running a home and trying to keep family contacts, together with all the responsibilities that accompany the caring role. It is no wonder the carer gets overwhelmed when unexpected complex situations arise, as was the case of Mrs Owens (below). Personalities often get highlighted in the process of dementia and, in Mrs Owens' case, her suspicious nature became paranoid.

The impact of caring can have a huge emotional toll on the primary carer. There can be ongoing loss and grief as the carer sees more and more deterioration in the person they are caring for, with loss of the person they once were. Roles become reversed; at times a son or

Owens said that "they had many an argument if any other lady paid any attention to me". Coming to terms with the current issues Mr Owen stated emphatically, "Nothing is different now she has Alzheimer's... that is her personality!"

A solution to this jealousy was found when the service supervisor referred the problem to a clinical nurse consultant. The nurse consultant met with Mr Owens and the young woman assigned to Mrs Owens' care. The young lady was included in the meeting so she became part of the solution and did not feel she was being treated rudely. Strategies were implemented as follows:

• The visit of care staff was to be made a 'non-event'
• No welcoming greeting from Mr Owens, the young woman was to let herself in and go about her duties as pleasantly as she always did but with minimum attention being focused on herself
• All communication was to be in the presence of Mrs Owens
• No conversations were to be held in a separate room; any care changes that could not be said in Mrs Owens' presence would have to be via telephone calls to the service supervisor
• The young woman was to see herself out, with no 'goodbyes' or 'thank you' from Mr Owens.

These strategies did achieve a good outcome: Mrs Owens settled down and her suspicion reduced. Mr Owens was pleased as he was becoming physically more frail and increasingly reliant on the assistance from the community service.

daughter can take on the parenting role, sometimes putting their own lives on hold with conflicting demands draining their energy and taking their time. This was the case for Mr and Mrs Harrison (see below).

Attending the local carer support group was very beneficial to Mrs Harrison and her family; she was directed to the right person who could approach the problem objectively and find a suitable solution. As discussed previously, carer support groups can be invaluable. Hopefully the information in this chapter may encourage all primary carers to attend. Phoning an Alzheimer's helpline will give information as to the time and venue of the nearest carer support group.

Case study: Mrs Polanski

Marked deterioration in social behaviour and speech; inability to find words, or names of people or objects.
86 years old, Mrs Polanski had been diagnosed two and a half years previously with vascular dementia but as time went by it was thought she had a mixture of that and Alzheimer's disease.

Presenting problem
Anti-social behaviour.

With marked deterioration in her health and daily function, compounded by the recent death of her husband, Mrs Polanski moved in with her daughter, Mrs Harrison and her husband. The mother and daughter had shared a close relationship previously but Mrs Harrison was becoming more and more frustrated with her mother as she was continually disrobing and wandering around the home and garden naked. This was occurring in the presence of the much embarrassed Mr Harrison, the neighbours and also when the grandchildren visited. Everyone was becoming very stressed about Mrs Polanski's anti-social behaviour.

The disrobing stressed the husband-wife relationship, especially when the grandchildren became upset by grandma's nudity. Mrs Harrison raised her problems at the support group she was attending, and input from an experienced clinical nurse consultant was sought.

Consideration was given to the possibility that maybe Mrs

Caring for a person living with dementia at home is not easy; carers can get very frustrated especially when they can no longer understand what the person is saying, or they repeat the same question or statement over and over again. It can wear the primary carer down. However, it is usually the 'below the belt' issues, inappropriate sexual behaviours, urinary or faecal incontinence that become the last straw for the carer. That is why it is essential, when these problems happen, that help is sought. Carer support group facilitators or an Alzheimer's helpline will direct the primary carer to the right resource, people or education material. It is necessary to appreciate that urinary or faecal incontinence are not inevitable companions of dementia – they usually occur in the later palliative stages when comfort measures are put in place.

Polanski's temperature control, centred in the hypothalamus, may have been rendered dysfunctional by dementia, leading Mrs Polanski to remove her clothing because she was feeling hot. An air conditioner, left on day and night, was tried but the disrobing continued.

The problem was, however, solved when it was suggested that a silk poncho be 'kept at the ready' to cover Mrs Polanski whenever she disrobed. It really was of no consequence that she had no underclothing on, the main issue was to retain her modesty which the poncho provided. Mrs Polanski didn't object to the poncho, she liked the 'sensuous' feel of the silk garment and happily wore it. A silk kaftan was also purchased and Mrs Polanski wore it on the occasions she went out. She relied on Mrs Harrison to dress her, because it was obvious that the process of dementia had robbed her of the correct dressing sequencing.

Mrs Harrison did eventually recall that neither her mother nor father wore night attire to bed. This habit probably originated in her early married wartime days back in Poland when clothing was rationed.

Appreciating that old habits were well entrenched in her mother's memory, instead of insisting on Mrs Polanski wearing pyjamas, Mrs Harrison decided the nudity was acceptable in bed and she provided her mother with a satin dressing gown to use upon rising. The satin produced another 'feel good' item of clothing for Mrs Polanski to wear and the disrobing ceased.

Dementia and Sexuality

When the caring role becomes unmanageable, it can be an extremely hard decision for the primary carer to transfer the care to a residential facility. Hopefully they will feel comforted by the thought that they can still be involved, even though the caring role has been transferred onto care staff. They can be in a more relaxed position to continue to visit and continue the 'loving' relationship.

CHAPTER FIVE

Establishing Connections

The aim of this chapter is to introduce the tried and tested PLISSIT model of care that can prove useful for residential care staff to connect with embarrassed or worried primary carers when issues about sexual expression arise.

'I've learned that people will forget what you said, people will forget what you did, but people will never forget how you made them feel.'

Maya Angelou (2009)

Dementia and Sexuality

When the ongoing care needed for the person living with dementia is transferred to an aged care residential facility, it is so important to have continual interaction with the person's primary carer(s). Inappropriate sexual behaviour may have been the cause for the primary carers not being able to cope at home and may not have sought help from community services. A primary carer is often bewildered, frustrated, embarrassed or troubled by the inappropriate behaviour. Commonly they have difficulty discussing it.

Often the primary carer will carry a burden of guilt, feeling that they have let their relative or friend down by accepting placement for them in an aged care facility. A common statement made by these carers can be:

> *"It is hard to come to terms with the changes in behaviour. Our 'loved one' has always been such a private person regarding sexual activities and they have never been so openly sexually expressive before. We feel so embarrassed"*

Such statements are a good opportunity for care staff to approach the primary carer, in a sensitive, empathetic manner, to ask if they would like to talk about the worries and feelings they are experiencing. If the primary carer is in agreement, the care staff need to find a private area that will provide a safe and relaxed forum to discuss the sexually expressive or overt behavioural problems that are of concern. Care staff also need to be aware and sensitive to the needs of a same sex partner who has cared for the person over many years. Their worries and issues are often neglected or pushed aside if family members come forward and want to take ownership of any decision making.

Sharing feelings can be a very emotional time for a primary carer and they need a lot of support. It is important the care staff member supporting them is comfortable with the topic. Sometimes this might be a good point to refer to an experienced staff member more skilled and confident to discuss the issues.

Nevertheless, whatever level of experience the care staff member has, they must establish a rapport with the primary carer(s). A very useful guide to open a comfortable communication channel is the tried and tested PLISSIT Model of Sexual Therapy (Annon, 1976). This model was first used, according to Rheaume *et al* (2008), "with young adults, but is now used to assess sexuality and guide intervention in older adults as well". In this application, Davis *et al* (2006) state, "it can provide a framework for intervention aiding healthcare professionals to address sexuality". I have modified it to guide interactive sexual discussion with primary carers and have found it to be a useful resource, initiating conversation and giving information in a logical sequence.

PLISSIT is an acronym (P-LI-SS-IT) for:
- Permission
- Limited Information
- Specific Suggestions
- Intensive Therapy.

Permission

In the first instance gaining 'permission' to discuss a person living with dementia's inappropriate sexual behaviour breaks down barriers to allow the care staff to focus on a primary carer's concerns, talking with and listening to the problems and worries they may be experiencing. Making the carer feel at ease and reassuring them that their feelings are quite normal needs to be projected in a friendly and caring way. This approach sets up a safe environment, helping open discussion.

Apart from the embarrassment a primary carer may feel, they may need to know more about the disease process. In some cases, especially when the primary carer is a son or daughter, they may see their parent forming a new relationship and feel the behaviour is beyond the consenting capacity of their mother or father. There can be pent up feelings of anxiety and even hostility they need to express. It is important to let the primary carer know that, despite a lot of myths and misconceptions, sexual desires and interests do continue throughout a person's lifespan. A person who finds themselves alone in a residential care facility and has previously shared a close sexually active relationship, even with the added diagnosis of dementia, will continue to seek intimate companionship. Indeed Kamel *et al* (2004) found "that sexual behaviour is normal and even beneficial on many levels".

Dementia and Sexuality

Case study: Mr Howard

Frontal lobe impairment.

76 years old, Mr Howard had been living with his daughter, Mrs Green, for the last two years after his wife had died. He was in the later stages of vascular dementia and required more assistance than his daughter could give so he had been recently admitted to a high care residential facility.

Presenting problem

Gross overt sexual behaviour: disrobing, exposing himself and masturbating in public areas.

After a settling-in period the presenting sexual problems surfaced, causing a lot of distress to the care staff, Mrs Green and other visitors to the facility because the overt masturbation was in communal areas for all to see.

During discussions, Mrs Green, even though she had given her 'permission' to talk over her father's inappropriate sexual problems, became very emotional and stated:

"The same problems were happening at home for the last six months before my father's admission to the residential facility. He has always been a 'gentleman' but to see the change in his behaviour has been very distressing. My father was exposing himself and barging in on our 15-year-old daughter and myself whenever we, undressed or dressed, took a shower or went to the toilet."

Mrs Green became even more emotional saying:

"I was unable to cope with such behaviour and that was the reason for the residential placement. I do not want my daughter to remember her grandfather as 'a dirty old man'. He was a good father and grandfather and I want the good image to be our lasting memory of a fine man!"

It helped Mrs Green greatly when she was given 'information' making sense of her father's behaviour. Reviewing the CAT scan image, taken before the residential placement, revealed that vascular damage had occurred in the frontal lobe of the brain. This created the opportunity to explain frontal lobe dysfunction and enabled Mrs Green to understand her father's loss of social and inhibitory skills.

During this session of sharing information Mrs Green was asked if she could recall anything that would suggest whether her parents were physically sexually active. She thought for a while and replied with a twinkle in her eye:

"I think they were very sexually active. They both had high-profile jobs and on the week-ends they used to give my sister and myself money to go to the movies on Saturday and again on Sunday, telling us not to hurry home. When I think about it, when we returned home both parents were both extremely happy and relaxed, very 'lovey dovey' I would say. Weekend nights in our home were very happy indeed!"

This valuable information from Mrs Green formed an important part of the problem solving process. As a result of the good empathetic rapport reached, Mrs Green, now relaxed and feeling at ease with the situation, was also able to give an account of her father's life, his occupation, likes, dislikes and hobbies. She revealed that her father had been a boxing trainer in his early days. This information was extremely useful too and was put to good use in the care planning process for him.

Specific suggestions given to Mrs Green to ensure her well-being were to:

- Continue with her regular visiting pattern in order to keep the close relationships that she had always shared with her father. Let the care staff do the 'caring' and she and her family continue to do the 'loving'
- Understand that she would always be consulted and have input into the ongoing care of her father
- Become a member of a carer support group. The education sessions and the carers' networking and exchange of coping strategies would be of big benefit to her
- Compile a scrap book for her father of his life's events. This would help reminiscence and open up a wealth of communication opportunities
- Give consent and financial support to engage the services of a remedial masseur to bring some comforting touch, now lacking in Mr Howard's life
- Feel free to consult with the care staff at any time about any concerns she or her family might have

Dementia and Sexuality

- Ask for professional help, which would include more detailed 'intensive therapy', if she still harboured any feelings of guilt about her father's residential placement.

Based on Mr Howard's boxing training past, which included "giving his boxers a good rub down with essential oils" before a fight, Mrs Green consented to the engagement of a remedial masseur. The masseur came twice weekly much to the delight and fond memories of Mr Howard. At the sight of the masseur Mr Howard willingly removed his shirt, laid on his bed, turned on his stomach and exposed his back, thus giving 'implied' consent to the massage. Implementing the comfort of touch into Mr Howard's care plan put an end to the overt masturbation. The photograph album that Mrs Green put together contained photos of Mr and Mrs Howard's early life together, which helped Mr Howard to re-live past pleasures. Mrs Green also put a tape recording together of her father's favourite melodies. As a result of these interventions his inappropriate behaviour ceased.

Mrs Green was greatly relieved to have been given the opportunity to express her concerns and be part of a process that enhanced her father's quality of living. On thanking the staff, she indicated at this point in time she would not require further consultative meetings; she now had an understanding of her father's anti-social behaviour and she was appreciative that she had been included, and would remain included, in planning his care needs.

Limited information

Providing 'limited information' initially is a good start to help the primary carer(s) understand the process of dementia and the impact it has on a person's sexuality. Giving them selected fact sheets or a pamphlet explaining dementia and sex-related issues helps the understanding process. This gives the primary carer time to absorb the information and ask related questions in follow-up meetings. It is important not to bombard the primary carer with too much reading material at first, as it can be overwhelming. Specific reading materials need to be added gradually later.

Giving details as to the location of dementia and memory resource centres, helpline services, counselling services and carer support groups in their area can be very helpful to the primary carer(s). It may be necessary to point out the advantages of attending a carer support group.

Specific suggestions

Whilst interacting with the primary carer, it can be a good idea to give a forecast of possible 'specific suggestions' that might be included in a care plan. Some of these can help bridge the gap of any unmet sexual needs. A 'specific suggestion' might include the use of sensory therapies, such as remedial massage, aroma or music etc. This is a good opportunity to ask the primary carer if there would be finances available if a remedial masseur was to be recommended.

Another suggestion would be to ask the primary carer if they would put a life story scrap book and photograph album together, as these items may be used later as part of a reminiscence distraction programme. The care worker needs to be aware of privacy and confidentiality issues if a relationship has been kept concealed for many years. A good suggestion made by Mackenzie (2009) would be to ask the partner "to create an autobiography containing a level of detail they feel most comfortable sharing later on in the journey through dementia".

Another 'specific suggestion' might be to invite the spouse or partner to stay overnight. This suggestion would have been helpful in the case of Mr and Mrs Darcy in Chapter 3, explaining to Mrs Darcy that a 'do not disturb' sign would be displayed on the door to ensure the couple's privacy. Another suggestion may be to plan, with the spouse's agreement, to take the person living with dementia home for an overnight stay. This might make the spouse anxious that the person living with dementia, once home, would not want to return to the residential care facility. Each relationship needs to be treated on its own terms.

Intensive therapy

Advising primary carer(s) of the availability of 'intensive therapy' from a dementia specific counselling service, Alzheimer's helpline counsellors, sex therapist, psychologist, social worker or a clinical nurse consultant

Dementia and Sexuality

who may be specialised in the field might be helpful to them. Contact details will need to be given. One-to-one counselling could be a good option to share their feelings or complicated problems in private with an independent listener.

Working their way through the modified interactive PLISSIT model guidelines gives the care staff an opportunity to reassure the primary carer(s) that they will always remain an integral part of the person living with dementia's life, including the planning of their future care and, where cognitively possible, this would include the person they had cared for.

Case study: Mrs Irwin
Frontal lobe impairment.
70 years old, Mrs Irwin was diagnosed with Alzheimer's disease, two and a half years previously. She was now living in a dementia-specific unit.
Presenting problem
Continual sexually expressive behaviour.

Mr Irwin visited Mrs Irwin every day. Mr Irwin's biggest embarrassment was that his wife continually wanted to engage in physical sex. Sensing Mr Irwin's uneasiness, the care staff member assigned to Mrs Irwin's care asked Mr Irwin for permission to talk about the situation. Mr Irwin agreed and was pleased to be able to unburden his problems. When asked about his and his wife's sexual history he stated:
"We both had a very fulfilling active sexual life together, but in the present circumstances I now feel that my wife, as a result of the Alzheimer's disease, really does not know what she is doing; disrobing, dragging me into her bed and continually wanting to fondle my private regions." He went on to say:
"I do not like the situation I find myself in. I am concerned that if I did engage in an intimate relationship with my wife, I really feel that in her present state I would be taking advantage of her."
During the consultation it was explained to Mr Irwin how Alzheimer's disease had affected Mrs Irwin's memory and daily living functions, especially her social and inhibition skills. Mr Irwin was given literature to read at home.

The case study starting on page 64 is a good example of a daughter's embarrassment when dealing with her father's overtly sexual behaviour, brought on by the progression of his dementia. However, by using the interactive communication guidelines of the PLISSIT model, a clinical nurse consultant was able to allay the daughter's anxiety and discomfort.

Another example of how helpful the use of the modified PLISSIT Model can be was shown in the case of Mrs Irwin (below).

Specific suggestions were made, inviting Mr Irwin to stay with his wife overnight occasionally. He was reassured that their privacy would be upheld. However Mr Irwin disclosed:
"I would feel embarrassed if I embraced my wife behind a 'Do not disturb' sign on the door. I would be conscious that staff would be aware and I would feel that they would be smirking at the old couple having sex."
As a result of Mr Irwin's apprehension, it was suggested that he should have more formal meetings with an experienced clinical nurse consultant. These encounters gave him more opportunity to unburden his feelings.
During these 'intensive therapy' sessions, it was noted that the couple had never worn night clothes to bed, so in actual fact Mrs Irwin's disrobing was a common occurrence in her long-term memory. The fact that the couple had always had a very close intimate relationship was also still embedded in Mrs Irwin's memory. Mr Irwin disclosed:
"Touching one another's private areas was, in the past, part of our foreplay."
Mr Irwin's disclosures showed that Mrs Irwin's behaviour had once been normal for the couple.
The consultant suggested he should take his wife home for a night and, whilst in the privacy of their own bedroom, share their intimate feelings and achieve sexual gratification. This proved very successful for the couple, and Mr Irwin's concerns reduced so much so that the overnight home stays became a regular occurrence.

Dementia and Sexuality

If care staff make sure they take the time to engage with the primary carer that is central to the life of the person they are now caring for, a positive interaction of benefit to all will be achieved.

Using the interactive PLISSIT model can be extremely useful to open up two-way communication. These guidelines can become, firstly, the foundation of a trusting relationship that benefits both primary carer(s) and the care staff. In particular the primary carers feel relieved that they can share the feelings which will help them understand why inappropriate sexual behaviour has occurred.

Secondly, the care staff have an opportunity to gather more problem solving information, especially sexual and life histories about the person they are caring for. Some primary carers, like Mrs Green (page 64), might not know a lot about a person's life-long sexual behaviour but might have enough information to give a few clues or offer opinions which would help put together an overall picture.

CHAPTER SIX

Addressing Ethical Dilemmas

The purpose of this chapter, first, is to create awareness about the ethical dilemmas, often originating from misunderstandings and prejudices, which challenge the person living with dementia's right to sexual expression. Secondly, to discuss the issues involved for a care staff member when an ethical dilemma may compromise their duty of care.

'Ethics is nothing else than reverence for life'

Albert Schweitzer

Dementia and Sexuality

Ethical dilemmas often arise when new relationships form in residential care settings. Care staff can become concerned when they see a male resident forming a liaison with a female co-resident who has dementia, even if both parties are widowed. Misunderstanding and even prejudices develop against the man involved. The care staff might feel they need to protect the woman, feeling that the man might be taking advantage of her impaired decision making and judgment.

The primary carer may experience these prejudices as well. As discussed in Chapter 5, it is often the sons or daughters that take exception to a new relationship forming, feeling their mother or father's capacity to make informed decisions regarding a new relationship is diminished because of their diagnosis of dementia. They worry, particularly in the case of their mother, whether she has been coerced into forming a relationship. They may ask for an end to be put to the relationship.

As a consequence ethical dilemmas can be created when interventions to terminate a relationship do not take into account the person living with dementia's own wishes – especially if they have implied consent by their actions, for example undressing and getting into bed with a co-resident. Questions always arise about the capacity of a person living with dementia to make an informed decision to enter into a sexual relationship. The Attorney General's Department of New South Wales, Australia (2008) defines legal capacity for an adult person "as the ability to make a decision for themselves; understanding the facts and choices involved, being able to weigh up the consequences and communicate the decision".

Within the United Kingdom, the issue of capacity and best interest is treated slightly differently within each country, however the principles of best interest remain essentially the same. In England and Wales the Mental Capacity Act 2005 supports the belief that a person has the capacity to make a specific decision unless proven otherwise; in Scotland the equivalent statute is the Adults with Incapacity (Scotland) Act 2000, while in Northern Ireland there is as yet no act governing this area and common law of best interest still applies (Nuffield 2009).

Therefore, according to Berger (2000), to make a specific decision to be sexually active the person is required to have capacity for insight, judgment and be able to appreciate the consequences of their actions.

Doubt as to the person living with dementia's ability to comprehend the decision making process may pressurise both family and care staff into compromising the person's autonomy. The 'consensual' sexual activity in question makes them feel anxious and uncomfortable (Metzger *et al* 2002 abridged). Archibald (2005) reports continual "anxiety or rebuke from families can mean residential care facilities veer towards protection and control rather than having a more liberal approach".

Kuhn (2002) poses some thought provoking questions that need to be considered in the context of the above issues:

- "To what extent should others be allowed to make decisions about the relationships of residents?
- Does anyone have a right to impose a code of behaviour as long as no laws are broken?
- Who decides and how?"

"Whilst mental capacity and competence are central to decision making," Kuhn (2002) states, "they should not be the sole determinants in the life of a resident with dementia. It is well recognised that persons with Alzheimer's disease typically retain a task-specific competence, even those with severe cognitive impairment. A resident may perform poorly on a mini-mental status test but his or her preference for a special friend or lover may be quite evident." This statement reinforces the principle in the legislation of the UK and the Attorney General's Department of NSW (2008) opinions that capacity is decision-specific. It can vary in different circumstances, at different times, and about different types of decisions. If a person can make some but not all decisions, then they have a right to make as many decisions as they can.

Staunton *et al* (2008) argue, "The existence of an illness or condition is not sufficient to remove the presumption that they have the capacity to make their own decisions." Even people with advanced dementia are

Dementia and Sexuality

capable of periods of insight and therefore have the capacity to be decision-specific. As Metzger *et al* (2002) explain, "An individual who must defer to his/her health care proxy a decision about a particular medical treatment may yet be able to make valid decisions about sexual relationships."

If the family or the care staff still feel ill at ease with the notion of decision-specific capacity, an assessment by a professional experienced in this field may be necessary. The assessor, whilst appreciating the person might not have the capacity to make decisions about some things, would ensure they may have the capacity to make other decisions. Therefore the assessor would have to ascertain whether the person, when making a 'decision-specific', had the ability to:

- "understand the facts involved
- understand the main choices
- weigh up the consequences of the choices
- understand how the consequences affect them
- communicate their decision" (Attorney General's Department of NSW, 2008).

In New South Wales, if an assessor does find the person incapable of making specific decisions, a substitute decision maker can be appointed by a guardianship tribunal. "A substitute decision maker should be the last resort, used only when all efforts to assist a person to make a decision for themselves have been unsuccessful," says the Attorney General's Department of NSW (2008). Similar systems apply in the UK, but may vary slightly in the process, and with whom the power lies to make decisions on behalf of another person (Mental Capacity Act, 2005; Adults with Incapacity, 2000). Practitioners are encouraged to refer to the legislation in their own particular country of practice.

The following case study is an example of the ethical dilemmas surrounding decision-specific 'implied' consent.

Case study: Mrs Andros

Perceived inappropriate behaviour.

75 years old, Mrs Andros has been living with Alzheimer's disease for the past three years. She recently moved to a residential care facility, following the death of her husband.

Presenting problem

Mrs Andros was seeking a new relationship with another resident, evidently enjoying his company and engaging in sexual activity with him, much to the concern of her daughter and care staff who felt Mrs Andros needed protection from her own impaired decision making and judgment.

Mrs Andros married young. She and her husband migrated from their Greek home to Australia in the mid '50s and the couple raised two children. Mrs Andros's daughter visited her mother regularly in the residential care facility. On learning that her mother had formed a sexual liaison with Mr Pollark, a widowed resident, she became very upset. Care staff reported that Mrs Andros continually sought out Mr Pollark's company and had been observed knocking on his bedroom door, taking her clothes off and getting into bed with him.

The daughter was concerned that her mother had no capacity to enter into this new relationship, even though her mother's actions, such as disrobing, implied her consent. The daughter expressed her fears that her mother's dementia would have made her vulnerable to the risk of sexual coercion and questioned Mr Pollark's motives. She also felt that her mother's behaviour was not in keeping with her character and previous private ways of sexual expression, and requested that the relationship be stopped. On the other hand Mrs Andros's son, who had been appointed as her enduring power of attorney (for financial decisions) and enduring guardian (overseeing health and lifestyle issues), did not seem very concerned by his mother's liaison. He actually felt happy that she had found a new companion. A conflict of views developed between the son and the daughter. The son was happy to 'leave things be' but the daughter was extremely emotional and insisted that her brother use his appointed authority to have the care staff intervene and end the activity.

Dementia and Sexuality

The above conflict posed an ethical dilemma for the son: if his mother was expressing clear choices by her actions and Mr Pollark was content with the arrangements, was it really in the couple's best interest to prevent their liaison? After all, if the liaison had taken place in the privacy of their own home it would have certainly have seemed more acceptable. So should it be denied now both parties were living in residential care? (Metzger *et al*, 2002).

The care staff and daughter argued that Mrs Andros really did not have capacity to consent to a sexual activity when she did not have the capacity to remember if she had a shower that morning.

In counter argument, it is necessary to appreciate that there are two memory storage pathways: short-term memory recalls the morning shower and long-term memory recalls sexual activity, albeit recalling sexual activity from the past. That is a completely different thing from whether or not Mrs Andros had the level of understanding necessary to consent to a sexual relationship. However, if a person has experienced a fulfilling intimate relationship throughout their younger life they may continue to seek a similar relationship in their old age. Dementia is no barrier to the need for companionship and closeness with others. Kuhn (2002) states "giving and receiving intimacy does not end with a diagnosis of Alzheimer's disease". This was probably what Mrs Andros was experiencing.

Reflecting on the issues Kuhn (2002) raised, do others have the right to take away Mrs Andros's choice as well as undermine her individual rights? Williams (2009) says "a fundamental legal and ethical principle is that of autonomy; self-determination or choice, and that includes the right to make mistakes or poor decisions". It would seem, therefore, that a person's autonomy should be not stripped from them as long as they do not make decisions that put them at risk of harm or were not in the person's best interests. It was noted that when Mrs Andros entered the relationship, she did so freely and without coercion. The relationship appeared to be a significant source of pleasure for both Mrs Andros and Mr Pollark.

Despite knowing about her mother's new pleasure, the emotional and distraught daughter still insisted that the couple be separated, continually stating "what would my father think?". The care staff convened a family meeting.

After lengthy discussion, and to resolve the conflict with his sister, the son agreed that the liaison be temporarily stopped until an experienced professional had assessed Mrs Andros's decision-specific capacity. It was decided that the couple could continue to meet in the communal sitting areas under the supervision of the care staff.

Mrs Andros and Mr Pollark's intimate actions were now curtailed under the scrutiny of the care staff. It was reported that they used to sit close together and hold hands. No one had really considered their feelings or autonomy, especially those of Mr Pollark who did not have dementia. He felt humiliated and embarrassed by all the negative vibes that were coming from the care staff and the other residents within the facility. He had always had a close loving relationship with his now deceased wife and was looking for friendship and companionship. He thought he had discovered a close connection with Mrs Andros.

Mr Pollark had talked over his relationship with his son who was happy that his father had found a new companion. A new companion Mr Pollark said "who had willingly lain beside him, cuddling, kissing, caressing, enjoying the closeness, sharing their thoughts and physical intimacy". This was extremely pleasurable and sexually fulfilling for both of them and he was now saddened and dismayed to learn that Mrs Andros's family had felt he was just taking advantage of her. This situation created a dilemma for him as well. Whilst he still had deep feelings for Mrs Andros, if her family remained so strongly opposed, he felt he would be forced to seek companionship and attachment elsewhere.

Fortunately, after a sensitive professional capacity assessment on Mrs Andros, it was documented that even with mild to moderate Alzheimer's disease, Mrs Andros had insight and had demonstrated that she did understand the facts and the choices she had in wanting the relationship with Mr Pollark to continue. She weighed up and showed an understanding of the consequences of the relationship, communicating her desire to liaise with Mr Pollark in the privacy of his room. The assessor compared Mrs Andros's current behaviour with her previous sexual activities and concluded there was no real evidence that she lacked decision-specific capacity to consent to the intimate relationship.

At a further family meeting the daughter reluctantly accepted the professional finding. The son felt there were more benefits than risks of harm to his mother and agreed that she should continue her relationship with Mr Pollark in the privacy of his room. As a consequence of the capacity assessment process the care staff gained a better understanding of decision-specific consent and put plans in place to ensure the couple had privacy and time to spend together.

It would also have been helpful if it had been suggested to Mrs Andros's daughter that she should attend a carer support group as well as seeking professional counselling to assist her overcome her anxieties. Care staff need to be mindful that, as Kamel et al's (2004) research suggests, "providing counselling to family members and educating them about the sexual needs of elderly persons may help avoid ethically challenging situations".

Another ethical dilemma that may arise and cause a lot of anxiety occurs when a gay, lesbian, bisexual transgender or intersex (GLBTI) older person living with dementia is admitted to a residential care facility. The dilemma centres on whether to disclose the person's sexual preference and lifestyle, or whether it is best for the person to remain 'closeted' masquerading as heterosexual. It will all depend initially on how welcome and comfortable the person (and their partner if they have one) is made to feel during the admission procedure, how sensitively the care staff approach the emotional time of entering permanent care. Past negative attitudinal experiences may have made GLBTI people sensitive to adverse comment. "This is not surprising," according to Barrett et al (2008), "given that many of these men and women grew up in an era when disclosure could result in enforced medical 'cures', imprisonment or loss of family, employment and friends."

Consequently, for the majority of older GLBTI people, hiding under a 'heterosexual' façade for most of their lives may have been protection from workplace scrutiny or homophobia. GLBTI people may also masquerade because of the "marginalization visited upon them if they chose to come out of the closet" (Nay *et al*, 2007). Nevertheless, "personal sexual orientation continues to be an important and integral part of a person's identity" (Mackenzie, 2009). Ward *et al* (2005) confirm that "sexual identity is fundamental to relationships, emotion, intimacy, attachment, self image and life experience. Consequently, in order to offer person-centred dementia care, a person's sexual orientation needs to be acknowledged".

However the person, or their partner, may feel uneasy as to how their sexual orientation would be received by heterosexual care staff if a display of affection or a decision to disclose their sexual preference was made. If this was the case they must be given the freedom not to discuss it if that is their wishes, in which case their sexual orientation will not be acknowledged. Keep in mind that any homophobic 'vibes', be it a judgmental look, shrug of the shoulders or raised eyebrows, may make the person or their partner "revisit past discriminatory experiences" according to Barrett *et al* (2008) and "consequently feel upset, anxious and depressed".

The Anti-Discrimination Act introduced in the United Kingdom in 1975 and in Australia in 1977 made it against the law to discriminate against someone on the basis of a person's gender or sexual orientation. Further legal structures to prevent discrimination in the UK were set in place via the Race Relations Act (1976) and the Race Relations (Amendment) Act (2000) to fight racism, and the Disability Discrimination Act (2005) to fight discrimination against disabled people. In England and Wales homosexuality was made legal via the Sexual Offences Act (1967) and in Northern Ireland via the Homosexual Offences (Northern Ireland) Order (1982). The Equality Act (2005) explicitly outlawed many forms of sexual orientation discrimination. Barrett *et al* (2008) write that in Australia "public agencies are obliged to consider that people have the right to enjoy their human rights without discrimination and the right to enjoy their identity and culture". In order to incorporate the above principles into residential person-centred dementia care and avoid residents "experiencing prejudice, ignorance or exclusion as a result of sexual preference", Knocker (2006)

Dementia and Sexuality

suggests, "the care staff need to seek education on the diverse needs of older GLBTI people living with dementia". Being aware of the diversity of these needs will help care staff "rethink automatic heterosexual assumptions when enquiring about a client's personal circumstances" (Price, 2008). "While automatic monitoring for sexual orientation might be contentious", Mackenzie (2009) suggests "having a conversation with a new client about who is the most important person in their life is likely to be met with less resistance". The importance and success of this approach was demonstrated by the case study below.

Case study – Miss Wentworth and Miss Kelly

De facto partners.
The two ladies had shared their lives for the last 36 years. They were inseparable but Miss Wentworth, living with vascular dementia for the past four years, had recently been admitted to a residential care facility.

Presenting problem

Miss Kelly was placed in an ethical dilemma: whether to disclose their private relationship, which she felt might be a betrayal of trust, or let it remain their secret.

Sixty-year-old Miss Wentworth had become totally dependent on Miss Kelly for all her daily living functions. Miss Kelly had previously rejected community services because their well kept secret would have been exposed with so many personal reminders of their intimate lifestyle spread throughout their home. Unfortunately, Miss Wentworth's now advanced vascular dementia made her personality changes all too obvious. She was easily upset, extremely anxious, unmotivated and at times depressed. Miss Wentworth was also becoming sexually disinhibited; hence the decision to seek professional care.

Miss Kelly felt that if she disclosed the couple's relationship, any staff homophobic vibes would accentuate Miss Wentworth's already dementia-compromised behaviour. Miss Kelly was well aware that with her partner's loss of social inhibitions she might inadvertently show her amorous attachment quite openly, thus making their sexual preference quite clear for all to see. This

An ethical dilemma of a different nature can arise when a care staff member may observe a fellow colleague sexually abusing a person entrusted to their care. Seeing something of this nature can cause significant concern and the staff member may feel some reluctance about reporting it. This abuse may come in many forms, for example in the way an enema is given, intentionally stimulating erogenous zones (nipples, breasts, genitalia) whilst attending to personal hygiene or when inserting a catheter or applying/changing a continence absorbent aid.

dilemma was playing on Miss Kelly's mind as she had managed to keep her own sexual identity very private for many years.

The two ladies were fortunate to have a network of friends of the same sexual orientation; these friends had become 'family'. Miss Kelly knew that they would certainly be visiting Miss Wentworth in her new abode and their continual visitations might raise eyebrows. Weighing all the factors involved and especially not wanting to wipe out the past close relationship that she, Miss Wentworth and their 'family' of friends had shared, Miss Kelly made the decision to disclose their sexual orientation.

Fortunately the residential care facility chosen for Miss Wentworth had an in-built philosophy of maintaining the person's individually, rights and choices. The admitting care staff were familiar with the diverse needs of GLBTI older people and their response to the disclosure was sensitive and accommodating. Miss Wentworth was allocated a private room and the 'family' network was welcomed. Miss Kelly was included in the person-centred care planning and an agreement was made that all Miss Wentworth's hygiene needs were to be attended to by female staff. As a result Miss Kelly's anxieties were laid to rest.

All residential care facilities need to have similar admission policies and procedures in place so they can assure the incoming resident and their prime carer that every effort is made to value the uniqueness of each individual, giving both GLBTI and heterosexual residents the same support and validation of their self worth and sexual identity. Then, and only then, will the dilemma of disclosure, as shown in this case study, become non-existent.

Dementia and Sexuality

The dilemma and reluctance to report a colleague's deviant actions to management may originate from worries about consequences such as being intimidated, harrassed, bullied or labelled as a 'whistle-blower' by the perpetrator or other staff members.

Every care staff member, nevertheless, has a duty of care to report such heinous actions. The person living with dementia's vulnerability, at times not knowing or appreciating the intent of what is being done to them or who is doing it, makes them an easy target for a 'sexually deviant' carer or staff member (Jeter, 2008). Failure to report such violations allows this abuse to continue unchecked.

Being the person's advocate, despite any rebound consequences, is essential to ensure the well-being and safety of the person entrusted to any care establishment. Documenting any tell-tale signs of sexual abuse such as unaccountable "bruising or bleeding around genital or breast areas, reluctance to be undressed or bathed" (Ozanne *et al*, 2009), or agitation when continence appliances are fitted or changed is essential. Documented evidence substantiates any claims that sexual abuse was observed.

Suspicions of more violent sexual abuse in the form of rape may be generated despite a lack of any real evidence, other than staff intuition, when the physical symptoms above are accompanied by unusual walking difficulties, pain when cautiously sitting and obvious genital trauma (McCreadie *et al*, 2006). As the person living with dementia is sometimes unable to speak up, rape can often go undetected for some time. The perpetrator can be a stranger (who crept into a bedroom unseen at night), care staff, family member or friend and even at times a spouse.

The media has reported over the past years that there have been reprehensible occurrences of rape and other forms of sexual abuse on vulnerable unsuspecting older females, particularly those living with dementia and residing in aged care facilities (Jamieson,1999, O'Neill, 2006, Metherell, 2006, Benson, 2008, Wallace, 2008). All such cases have required, and current cases still do require, police investigation and criminal charges to be laid once the perpetrator is found.

Bearing in mind the profound effect of sexual abuse on an individual person, any suspicious circumstances should be reported immediately to the management team. Staff will find that each health care, community, aged care service or facility will have their own policies in place to assess and support allegations of suspicious circumstances indicating any form of sexual abuse. Alternatively, a referral can be made to an aged care advocacy service or the equivalent for advice on these matters.

In concluding this chapter, three different types of ethical dilemmas have been used to demonstrate the complex situations that could occur in day to day care and interaction with people living with dementia and their primary carer/s. Care staff need to keep in mind that ethical dilemmas are always challenging, involving moral values and judgment. Personal codes of conduct and some conflict of interest may occur, not only for the person and the concerned 'significant others' but for themselves as well.

To address the complexity of the first two case studies, the person living with dementia's wishes, rights and capacity to make 'specific' decisions have to be taken into account, as well as respecting individual's autonomy, privacy, dignity and diversity.

The third ethical dilemma centred on the care staff member's personal issues with reporting a colleague for sexual abuse and the need to speak out against such malpractice. In this instance 'duty of care' and being an advocate to ensure the safety, security and well-being of the person entrusted to their care have to override such concerns.

PART THREE

Discovering Solutions

'Too often we underestimate the power of touch, a smile a kind word, a listening ear, an honest compliment, or the smallest act of caring, all of which have the potential to turn a life around'

Leo Buscaglia

CHAPTER SEVEN

Embarking on a Problem-Solving Pathway

This chapter includes a six-step problem-solving pathway, helpful in uncovering the origins of a perceived problem, setting goals, planning and evaluating person-centred care, and addressing education needs as they arise.

'Each problem that I solved became a rule, which served afterwards to solve other problems'

Rene Descartes

The problem-solving process affords an opportunity to make a difference

How can care staff begin to overcome what is perceived to be inappropriate behaviour and facilitate ways that support sexual expression or rechannel it into desirable outcomes? It is a challenging situation! However before contemplating the task, the first step in the problem-solving pathway is to reflect for a moment what it would be like to have dementia.

The person living with dementia's world of reality suddenly becomes totally confusing for them and certainly miles away from the one known to care staff. Past and present time zones become jumbled together. Unable to think clearly, the person becomes easily disorientated even, at times, in a familiar environment. Memory deficits are common and memory can be present one minute and absent the next. Short-term memory is the first to go so words or statements are constantly repeated in an effort to stay 'on track'. Familiar faces, spouses or family members, may be misidentified, especially if there is an agnosia present, resulting from damage to the parietal lobe, described in Chapter 3.

Emotions can also flare up at times. A person living with dementia can quickly pick up on negative feelings that could stem from a care staff member's tone of voice, body language or rough handling (albeit unintentional; for example trying to get an unwilling person into the shower). The person will remember the negative feelings and react accordingly. Feil (1993) explains "anxious, agitated, aggressive outward behaviour is often a result of inner turmoil". A person living with dementia may have bursts of insight, they know something is wrong but they do not know how to rectify it because their dementia has caused damage to their thought processes as well as other functions of their brain.

As a result of this damaging process, the person is unable to comprehend or change their behaviour at the request of care staff. It will be ineffective just to tell the person living with dementia that their suggestive sexual advances are unwanted or that their sexual drives, desires or loss of inhibitions are inappropriate. These words will have no meaning to them and they will continue to replicate their behaviour. Therein lies the problem! Solutions have to be found to overcome this challenging situation.

Dementia and Sexuality

Unfortunately, when it comes to problem solving, barriers get put up because most people still think of a problem as a difficult or unpleasant situation, especially if it is identified as inappropriate sexual behaviour. Rusbult (2001) approaches a problem in a more positive way. He views a problem as "a situation where you have an opportunity to make a difference, to make things better; and problem solving is converting an actual current situation (the NOW-state) into a desired future situation (the GOAL-state). Whenever you are thinking creatively and critically about ways to increase the quality of life, you are actively involved in problem solving".

Embarking on a problem-solving approach will require the care staff to put behind them any previous negative experiences and assess the current situation objectively and in a sensitive manner, mindful also of the old adage "a problem is only a problem when it is perceived as a problem".

The following six-step pathway is a logical and helpful way to put the problem into context and work through to achieve a successful outcome:

1. Identifying the problems/issues
2. Diagnosing the problem
3. Setting goals and planning care around the individual's unmet needs
4. Implementing life enhancing strategies
5. Addressing education needs as they arise
6. Evaluating the outcomes.

1. Identifying the problem

During this investigative period, the care staff will need to adopt the role of detective because much questioning is involved in this first step. Initially it has to be made clear who has the problem. Does it belong to the person living with dementia or is it a problem held by the care staff? Very often it is a problem perceived by the staff; deemed or assumed to be 'inappropriate sexual behaviour'.

The next line of questioning is to discover what the perceived inappropriate behaviour actually is. Therefore, there is a need to ask whether it is:

- Disrobing
- Masturbation
- Unwelcome touching, gestures or suggestive language
- Wandering into another person's bedroom and getting into their bed uninvited
- Liaising with a co-resident who is not a spouse perhaps while the spouse visits daily.

There may be other behaviours reported that are not listed above, but whatever the actual behaviour is, it needs to be well documented as this information becomes part of the problem solving process.

2. Diagnosing the problem

A further line of questioning is needed, exploring:

a. Why is the person behaving this way?
i. Could they be physically ill?
ii. Are they demonstrating evidence of sexual frustration?
iii. Is there an obvious inability by care staff to respond to the situation?

b. How often, when or where is the behaviour a problem? Is the behaviour
i. Continuous?
ii. Worse at night?
iii. Happening in public?
iv. In the bathroom when being helped with bathing or toileting?

c. What is it that the person is doing?
i. Do they pinch, touch the private areas of care staff?
ii. Do they resist having their clothing removed? Refuse to be showered? (Keep in mind this could well be an indicator of a past sexual abuse experience especially for the individual who may have been subjected to wartime sexual exploitation or even cultural rituals).

Dementia and Sexuality

d. How does the person living with dementia feel about the situation? (Use observation skills if necessary). Is the person
i. Lonely?
ii. Bored?
iii. Separated from their spouse/partner and missing them?

e. How do care staff, primary carer or significant others feel? There is a need to document:
i. Whether care staff feel discomfort or disdain
ii. Whether the primary carer or significant other experiences embarrassment, distress or hostility
iii. Whether other co-residents feel discomfort, embarrassment or hostility
iv. Whether visitors show discomfort or condemnation.

f. What part of the brain is affected by dementia?
i. Is there loss of inhibition and moral judgment due to frontal lobe involvement?
ii. Is there another lobe that may be causing the problem?
iii. Is there multiple lobe involvement?
To find answers to these questions there may be a need to refer to the medical diagnosis and if possible the reports from any diagnostic tests such as specific scanning or magnetic resonance imaging (MRI) that may have taken place.

g. Are there any overriding physical conditions that could influence behaviour? Is there
i. Pain?
ii. Constipation?
iii. Infection, especially urinary?
iv. Side effects from medications or any other physical problems that are likely to affect the person's well-being?
Any or all of these conditions will need to be attended to immediately.

Care staff need to be particularly vigilant for signs of sexual abuse, especially unexplained bleeding or bruising around breast or genital regions. Keep in mind that older women are at greater risk of infection due to hormonal changes at menopause, which increase the likelihood of vaginal tears and abrasions during intercourse (Hillman, 2007). Special attention needs to be given to pain assessment as it often goes unreported because the individual may have difficulty explaining it. It may also affect their approach to sexuality.

   h. What was the person living with dementia's previous life and sexual history?
     i. What is the person's sexual orientation?
     ii. What were their known interests, hobbies, likes and dislikes?
     iii. Was there a lifetime of intimate relationships?
     iv. What was the previous pattern of sexual activity?

An effective way to gain a measure of the person living with dementia's present or previous level of sexual expression or physical sexual activity, is to remember that different people have very different levels of sexual drive throughout their lives (see the bell curve figure overleaf), and that most people's physical sexual activity lies in the middle of the curve. The good news is that they can continue to remain there, even in old age, as long as they do not have an overriding medical condition causing impotence or loss of libido. Others can be at either end; high or low in their sexual activity. These extreme ends can lead to labelling the person; 'dirty old man or woman', 'sexual deviant', 'randy' or 'nymphomaniac' at the high end, and labels such as 'frigid' or 'iceberg' at the low end.

If the person with dementia is unable to recall or depict where they sit on the bell curve, the primary carer may have some ideas/memories of past activity. It does need to be appreciated that the current bell curve position may show a marked swing to the high end with any disinhibition/dysfunction being emphasised as the dementia progresses.

Dementia and Sexuality

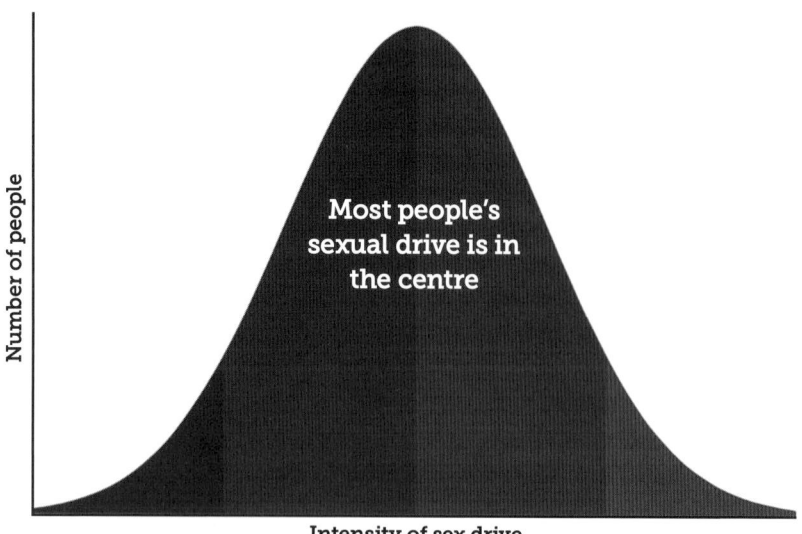

Bell curve showing the average distribution of sexual drive within the general population (Blanch, 1990)

3. Setting goals and planning care around the individual's unmet needs

Obtaining all the factual information, as discussed in steps 1 and 2 above, enables the perceived problem/s to be put into perspective and is central to individual goal setting and planning appropriate interventions. Bearing in mind the cognitive decline of the person living with dementia, including the loss of inhibitions, the setting of individual goals has to be achievable and meaningful. However, for any plan to be successful it has to be supported at managerial level; therefore it is important to keep management informed.

An understanding of the person's life profile is essential. The 'facade of dementia' has to be seen through to uncover the real identity, the core essence of the person, the who the person is and the who they have been. Once the person's profile, likes, dislikes, hobbies, past and present occupations and previous sexual history is known, individual goal setting and planning care can be started.

Care staff have identified the most challenging sexual behavioural problems that they find difficult to address as:

a. Disrobing and exposing genitalia
b. Masturbating in public
c. Unwanted sexual advances, verbal and non-verbal gestures understandably viewed by some as sexual harassment
d. Misidentification of faces, images, verbal meaning and the environment.

Goals set to overcome this unwanted behaviour, and support or rechannel sexual expression in an appropriate manner, aim to:

• Maintain the person's identity and well being
• Preserve the person's dignity
• Respect the person's privacy
• Initiate preferred sensual therapies (aroma, remedial massage, pets as therapy, dance, music and art for example)
• Redirect the person's inappropriate sexual drives to meaningful activities.

Well-planned interventions designed around the above goals can make a real difference to the stress and frustration levels of both the person living with dementia and the care staff (examples of these interventions will be given in the next chapter). There are a lot of life-enhancing care options but they have to be the ones best suited for the individual's needs and interests. Using one or a combination of the options listed below is an effective therapy to promote comfort, maintain individuality, provide alternative and meaningful sensory stimulation and activities as well as improve social relationships. Possible therapies include:

• Reminiscence
• Validation
• Sensory stimulation
• Individualised activities
• Use of sexual aids if appropriate.

Dementia and Sexuality

4. Implementing person-centred life enhancing strategies

One or several of the above interventions may be helpful to support sexual expression or rechannel the perceived inappropriate behaviour in other directions. It is a trial and error situation, and what works for one person will not necessarily work for another. Each intervention therapy has its merits and is worth a trial period. Successful interventions should be documented and included in the person-centred care plan.

A reminiscence approach is certainly useful to maintain the person's identity and well-being. Implementing the use of photograph albums, scrap books and memory boxes can connect the person to their past life experiences, joys, sorrows, relationships and levels of intimacy. It gives the care staff an opportunity to build a rapport with the person, share feelings and to validate the uniqueness of the person. Reminiscence combined with validation techniques maintains the person's identity and promotes their self-respect and self-worth.

The use of validation techniques is effective because they are "aimed to reawaken feelings of self-worth through self-awareness and accomplishments" according to Feil (1972) who also states, "sharing feelings allows entry to another's world and promotes interaction between one human being and another". Successful use of these techniques can help give care staff a positive regard for the person, affirming the value of who they are and who they have been; helping to identify their many life's accomplishments. Accomplishments could include 'rearing four children in the war years', or 'sewing their clothes when materials were rationed', or 'being a good provider for their family'.

An effective therapeutic intervention can be the use of sensory stimulation incorporating any one or a combination of the five major bodily senses including aromatherapy, remedial massage, pet therapy, dance, music, interactive feel and taste, as well as visiting a dedicated multisensory room utilising light, movement and sound if available. Pleasurable visual stimuli can relax a person living with dementia – for example, showing a DVD of a beautiful sunset, waterfalls or beautiful gardens, at the same time as having a nice perfumed bowl of flowers on display. Any form of these stimuli can fill the gaps in the 'sensuous' side of the person's sexuality.

Aromatherapy can be effective for some people. The healing properties of aromatherapy, according to Holt *et al* (2009), "are claimed to include promotion of relaxation and sleep, relief of pain and reduction of depressive symptoms; the rationale being that the essential oils have a calming and de-stressing effect". Holt *et al* (2009) add "it has been used for people with dementia to reduce disturbed behaviour". It is not yet scientifically proven, but I have found, in accordance with Holt *et al*'s research, that the use of essential oil of lavender or sandalwood (the latter a more earthy fragrance for males) can be effective in calming and settling unwanted inappropriate behaviour. Applying three drops of essential oil of lavender in a footbath or 8 drops in a full bath, after the water is run, can be very relaxing.

Remedial Massage Therapy, in the form of hand, shoulder or body massage, can be a comforting form of gratification as Bush's (2001) research found: "The comfort of human touch may be useful in decreasing agitated behaviours, improving sensory stimulation levels, inducing relaxation and increasing interrelatedness with the environment among cognitively impaired older adults." To initiate a programme including remedial massage, care staff will first have to ask the person for permission to touch. It needs to be noted that 'touch' may not always be welcomed as people have a personal space and it is up to them who they share this space with. There is an intimate space for 'lovers', more often an arm's length space for family and friends, as well as a more distant public space. Respecting a person's space is an essential part of care.

Pet therapy can be beneficial, especially to previous pet owners. Connecting old memories of caring for a pet can initiate some warm loving feelings and comforting gratification for a lonely, bored or anti-social person. Soft furry toy animals can be used in the same way; they can be held close, cuddled and loved.

Dance is useful in bringing about interactive closeness and touch as well as being good physical exercise. Douglas *et al* (2004) state, "It is relevant to note that this may also fulfil a need for non-sexual physical contact which many people with dementia find soothing".

Dementia and Sexuality

Music has been part of most people's lives. It can stir past memories and associations. Music activates, according to Banks (2009), "a sense of 'remembered self' and creates relaxation, a return to fond memories and feelings of calm and security". Brucsia (2009) believes "music and songs bear witness to our lives, connecting us to our inner world and giving voice to our experiences". This form of therapy is very good when it is combined with reminiscence and dance. Bright (1997) explains, "When words are gone, familiar early learned melodies return. These memories are stored forever in the brain's circuit. People living with dementia can sing or hum and foot tap to the tune and get a lot of relaxing pleasure and social engagement from music." As a consequence anti-social behaviour will usually reduce.

Art as therapy can bring out the creative side of a person and can be useful to rechannel behaviour perceived as inappropriate and get them thinking in other directions. Baines (2007) reveals "watching a person with dementia painting or writing is to be filled with awe, for, regardless of memory loss, the person is expressing and revealing a unique identity".

Implementing *meaningful activities* can stimulate remote memories, reconnecting the person to their previous roles, interests and hobbies. Engaging a person in something that is meaningful to them will rechannel their 'focus', give pleasure, re-establish dignity and increase the person's self respect. When a person is happy the inappropriate behaviour is usually forgotten. Verity (2010) suggests "the true focus is not about the activity itself but the quality and joy of the interaction".

Activities most commonly found to be effective are card games, dominoes, floral decoration, exercise programmes including those done from a chair, as well as organised social interactive occasions. Outdoor interests can be a useful distraction from a person's sexual drives. These can include gardening, walking or hydrotherapy for those able. "Making beauty salons and cosmetic services available for residents," according to Hajjar (2004), "may help them feel physically attractive and sexually desirable." Having someone wash and brush your hair or massage your scalp can be very sensuous. Having nails manicured is also another form of 'comforting touch'. The same comfort can apply for males who have someone else attend to their facial shaving.

Doll Therapy, whilst viewed by some people as demeaning, can be beneficial for people living with dementia, used therapeutically. Through interaction with a life-like doll, the person can relate to their early days of caring for their baby or babies. This therapeutic use can help the person to redirect and express their emotional feelings in another way, triggering the caring maternal or paternal inner self.

Setting up *private intimate opportunities* with a visiting spouse or partner, wherein the partner is given privacy and made to feel welcome and comfortable in this situation, is important as an intimate sexual activity which can reduce anxiety caused by spouse/partner separation. There are also surprising health benefits according to Doheny (2010) as physical sexual activity can "promote relaxation, reduce high blood pressure, improve insomnia, boost self-worth, reduce prostate cancer risk and improve female pelvic floor muscle tone". The latter improvement will also help maintain female urinary continence.

Sexually enhancing aids used in privacy might be a problem solving solution. Aids include vibrators for females used in conjunction with lubricating gel, vacuum pumps for male erectile problems, hiring a surrogate partner or enjoying watching sexually explicit magazines or X-rated DVDs. It is good practice to ask the person first if they have been in the habit of using any of these aids or services. The care staff will also need to be sure the person cognitively knows the purpose, preparation, application and cleanliness accompanying the use of these aids, or how to practice 'safe sex' if a surrogate partner is engaged. This is because "older people are more likely to unwittingly engage in unprotected sex" (Brock *et al*, 2007; Cloud *et al,* 2003; Hillman, 2007), not fully understanding the risk factors of Aids or HIV. A thorough assessment regarding the suitability of such aids or service is therefore always needed. There may very likely need to be a discussion of the appropriateness of the use of these aids with family and care staff.

There are so many options to help the person sustain or rechannel their sexual expression in meaningful ways. By using any one of these options, medications to make the person more docile or chemically castrate them are less likely to be needed.

5. Addressing education needs as they arise

Whilst formal education programmes are essential, the importance of bedside practical education should never be underestimated when obvious opportunities arise. Explaining the reasons why a person living with dementia overtly masturbates is a good example of such education. Lack of understanding of this problem continually produces feelings of distain and frustration for both the care staff and the primary carer. They complain that it is one of the most offensive situations to deal with. This situation can often be used as a teaching opportunity by challenging the complainants to ask themselves "why do people living with dementia masturbate in public view?" Once they have thought about the question, their conclusions usually are:

- Loss of environmental awareness due to parietal lobe damage
- Loss of moral judgement arising from frontal lobe damage
- Sexual expression
- Self-gratification or sexual stimulation
- Pleasure and relaxation
- Reduction of stress
- Making them feel good
- Relief of boredom
- 'Scratching' themselves
- Comfort of touch.

Focusing on the latter 'comfort of touch' can explain the reasons why the introduction of remedial massage therapy can relax and comfort the person, and as a consequence their behaviour, more often than not, improves. As an alternative to remedial massage the person who seeks his own comforting pleasure through masturbation needs to be given a private room, soap, 'washer' towel and a bowl of warm water in order to cleanse him/her self.

When making specific plans to implement remedial massage, the clinical educator needs to explain the benefits of it. A lot of people have their own connotations about the word 'massage'. A common reaction from care staff or primary carers might be, "we know all about what goes on in those massage parlours!". To put these ideas to rest, it is always best to emphasise the word 'remedial' explaining that remedial massage is a professional therapeutic treatment.

Education applied in this practical way in the workplace or the home setting will often have more meaning for the recipient. Hopefully they will remember a particular problem solving practice from the past and implement it in similar circumstances.

6. Evaluating the outcomes

The evaluation process is of great importance to any problem solving pathway. A valuable criteria and measurement of outcome is gathering the following information:

Level of comfort
- Is the person living with dementia more physically and emotionally settled?
- Has there been a reduction in care staff frustration or negativity?
- Is the primary carer or significant other(s) pleased that the person they care for has had their dignity and well-being restored?
- Do the co-residents or their visitors feel at ease with the situation?

Continuum of care
- Were the life-enhancing goals met?
- Is the person-centred care plan in place and working well?
- Were the implementations of the care plan supported at managerial level?

Education opportunities
- Was there a need for 'on the spot' education to address specific issues?
- What were the topics on which education was required?
- Were the topics recorded for inclusion into future formal education programmes?
- How many care staff were involved in the education and did they benefit?

Dementia and Sexuality

All answers to the above questions need to be documented, as they add to the success of the problem solving process as well as providing topics for inclusion in future in-service or education courses. If there are indications from the feedback that the problem solving was not successful, the whole process needs to start again. Identification of the problem and diagnosis of the condition may be the same but the goal setting and planning may need to be reassessed and other individually designed strategies implemented.

A wealth of information, identification of both the person's life profile and sexual history, can be easily generated when the line of questioning set out in the initial steps of the problem solving pathway is followed. In an endeavour to put the theoretical side of the problem solving pathway into workable practice, a series of case studies in the following Chapter 8 will demonstrate the benefits and successful use of some of these pathway options.

CHAPTER EIGHT

Putting it All Together

The purpose of this chapter is to demonstrate, using four different case studies, how laterally thinking problem-solving interventions, designed around person-centred unmet sexual needs, can support or rechannel perceived inappropriate behaviour into meaningful, life-enriching activities.

I am only one, but still I am one. I cannot do everything, but still I can do something. And because I cannot do everything, I will not refuse to do the something that I can do'

Helen Keller

Dementia and Sexuality

Alot of individual assessment, goal setting and creative planning is required to put together sexually enhancing strategies that will enrich the person's 'world of dementia'. Individual strategies, either to support or rechannel sexual expression, have to take into account the person's emotional status, their unmet sexual needs as well as the person's past interests and activity preferences. It is all about enriching the 'quality of living' for the person with dementia; making them feel good about themselves and valuing their identity, attributes and life experiences.

However, these strategies are not easy to implement in busy workplaces which have competing priorities. Continual intrusive inappropriate sexual behaviour can become very frustrating for staff, especially if they are not equipped with the required knowledge and skills to support, rechannel or redirect the problem behaviour.

In order to demonstrate how an effective outcome can be achieved using the problem solving pathway discussed in the previous chapter, four different case studies have been used.

Case Study – Mr Jonetti
Frontal lobe disinhibition.
65 year old, Mr Jonetti was diagnosed with Pick's disease. He had been caring for himself in his own home following the death of his wife, but his daily functioning had deteriorated in the last few months and he had recently been admitted to a dementia-specific unit.
Presenting problem
Inappropriate 'intimate touching'.

Much to the disdain of the care staff Mr Jonetti was observed approaching a particular female, who had advanced dementia, sitting her on his knee and placing his hand on her genitalia. He also took her hand and placed it on his own genitalia.

This act earned Mr Jonetti a label as a 'sexual deviant'. What concerned the care staff most of all was the fact that the female in question did not seem to be coerced, she was not objecting to the intimate touching. Nevertheless some of the exasperated care staff still felt Mr Jonetti was taking advantage of the lady's dementia. With these concerns in mind the care staff sought the problem solving skills of a clinical nurse consultant.

Following questioning, it became apparent that the care staff felt Mr Jonetti was probably bored and frustrated with his new environment. They identified that his objectionable behaviour was always in public, in the communal sitting room, which offended the other residents as well as their visitors. The care staff had every reason to feel uncomfortable and concerned and they did acknowledge that it was their problem to solve.

A friend was able to reveal some of Mr Jonetti's background. Migrating with his wife to Australia from Florence, Italy following World War II, he was employed as a bricklayer with a building firm. There were no children. As a consequence he and his wife became very involved with their local Italian social club, enjoying the regular card playing, social 'sing-a-longs' and dance nights. When Mrs Jonetti died ten years ago, Mr Jonetti continued to enjoy these evening activities. He had always been physically sexually active and enjoyed female company, so now in his widowhood, he continued to pursue this interest. He was always 'chatting-up' the ladies and inviting them back to his home, thus earning the reputation at his club, of being a 'Latin lover'. The friend, when shown the bell curve chart, felt that Mr Jonetti would have been at the very high end of the curve.

On reflecting on Mr Jonetti's medical diagnosis of Pick's disease, an understanding of the problem(s) began to be possible. Pick's disease stems from damage to the frontal and temporal lobes of the brain resulting in diminished social standards and judgment. It seemed likely therefore that Pick's disease was the reason for Mr Jonetti's anti-social behaviour. It was clear, too, Mr Jonetti had no insight that his behaviour was unacceptable.

Acknowledging Mr Jonetti's background, sexual history and his leisure interests, the following person-centred plan was implemented:

Liaison was established with the local Italian club to organise a volunteer visiting programme to help rechannel Mr Jonetti's behaviour by engaging in past meaningful activities and remi-niscence techniques:

Dementia and Sexuality

- Playing cards
- Familiar 'sing-a-long' sessions on a piano accordion
- Dancing to the music
- Compiling a scrapbook with scenes of Florence, holiday places which Mr and Mrs Jonetti had visited as well as the historical buildings of Rome
- Using a photograph album to recall happy occasions
- Remedial massage was begun twice weekly with a male masseur.

Whilst the remedial massage therapy brought comfort and touch into Mr Jonetti's life, helping him to relax, it was re-uniting him to the Italian community that changed Mr Jonetti's behaviour. The familiar music and dance, plus the other activities, reconnected Mr Jonetti to his past. According to Coaten (2001), "Reminiscence is a way of giving back to the person something of themselves that is precious... The process appears not be about re-enacting a past event or memory so much as re-living it in the present." A mixture of male and female volunteers, each person adding a new dimension to Mr Jonetti's life, gave him a lot of pleasure; so much so that he stood at the door each morning waiting for his visitor(s), forgetting all about his previous activities. The music and dance also brought a lot of pleasure and relaxation to co-residents as well because they were invited to join in.

Case study – Mrs Knight
Short term memory & thought processing deficits.
85 year old Mrs Knight had a long standing diagnosis of Alzheimer's disease and had been living in a high dependency unit for the past four years. Recently she had formed a close intimate liaison with a co-resident, Mr Manning.
Presenting problem:
Daughter's opposition to her mother's newly formed intimate relationship.

Mrs Knight's daughter, Mrs Lewis, complained to the care staff that it was unacceptable behaviour for her mother to be liaising with Mr Manning. Mrs Lewis was very hostile about the reported displays of affection. The couple were inseparable, always seen hand in hand and at times observed cuddling and kissing each other in full view of other residents. Mrs Lewis felt her mother's behaviour was uncharacteristic; her mother had always kept her emotions to herself. The care staff acknowledged that they were responsible for the 'co-liaison' problem.

Mrs Lewis agreed to attend a meeting, giving permission to work through the perceived problems, issues and concerns with the case manager and a clinical nurse consultant. This meeting enabled an exchange of information about Mrs Knight's life and sexual history that proved useful in working towards an amiable solution.

It was established that Mrs Knight was 42 years old when her husband died suddenly from a heart attack. Mrs Lewis was adamant that her mother had never looked for another relationship until now. Mrs Lewis was shocked when asked if her mother practiced masturbation. "My mother would never do that," she emphatically replied. Doubt was raised as to whether Mrs Lewis would really know what her widowed mother would do in private; explaining that, for some people, in the absence of a partner, masturbation can be a natural part of sexual expression.

A second meeting was arranged and on this occasion both daughter and mother were present. During the course of the meeting Mrs Knight sat silently by, until she saw a 'life-like' doll sitting on a nearby chair. The doll obviously rekindled a past emotional response and she picked it up, enthusiastically cuddling it, undressing and dressing it again, much to the surprise of her daughter.

This action triggered Mrs Lewis's memory of her mother's nurturing love of babies and young children. It was then revealed that her mother was always occupied with her home duties, never returning, after her marriage, to her previous employment as a shop assistant. However, she did become a 'paid carer' for her three daughter's children whilst the daughters worked. She loved to be useful and needed by others in this way.

Dementia and Sexuality

She had always welcomed minding a friend's or neighbour's baby when the need arose.

When asked to indicate her mother's previous sexual activity on the bell curve chart, Mrs Lewis inferred, as far as she knew, her mother would have always been on the low side. However, taking into account her newly formed relationship with Mr Manning it could appear, with the progress of dementia, that Mrs Knight had swung to the higher side. It was the dramatic change from her mother's once reserved nature to her current need for Mr Manning's company that made Mrs Lewis concerned.

Out of respect for Mrs Knight's well-being, a decision-specific capacity assessment was conducted. This assessment agreed that because of Mrs Knight advanced Alzheimer's disease she did not have the capacity, judgment, insight, or cognitive ability to understand the consequences of her actions. It was rationalised that perhaps Mrs Knight had responded to Mr Manning's attentiveness because her memories had taken her back to her nurturing role when she could freely express her emotions. Nevertheless, Mrs Lewis, who had enduring guardianship for Mrs Knight's care and welfare decisions, insisted that the liaison be stopped in an effort to preserve her mother's dignity.

As Mrs Knight had shown so much interest in the life-like doll, the use of doll therapy as a diversion strategy was put to Mrs Lewis. She was opposed at first, feeling the use of a doll would be demeaning to her mother. However she changed her mind when it was pointed out that the use of dolls in dementia care, especially in her mother's case, could help her to feel needed, useful and give her an opportunity to reconnect to her past caring role. According to Verity (2010), "Doll therapy has a strong symbolic meaning, providing purpose and nurture; it can help improve the overall well-being of the person with dementia".

Mrs Lewis purchased a 'life-like' doll, a cradle and all the accompanying equipment necessary. Plans were put in place for the doll to be treated as a real baby and this occupied Mrs Knight's attention day and night. Caring for the doll enabled Mrs Knight in her mind's eye to relive a time according to Verity (2010), "when she was a mother taking care of her children, giving and receiving love". Mrs Knight was often observed asleep cuddling the doll as she had done with her children so many years previously.

Mrs Knight became completely engrossed in her newly created 'mother' role. The close relationship with Mr Manning was a thing of the past. Unfortunately, however, this was not a good outcome for Mr Manning who was forced to seek companionship elsewhere. However, the care staff were very thoughtful and diverted his attention into other social engagements, outings and activities that had meaning and interest for him.

Case study – Mr Nelson
Frontal and temporal lobe damage; loss of social inhibitions.
58 year old, Mr Nelson was diagnosed with a younger onset dementia. He was still able to live alone in a self-care unit, situated within a retirement village. He received daily showering assistance from the village's care staff.

Presenting problem
Inappropriate touching, unwanted sexual advances and overt masturbation.

Care staff reported that each day, whilst helping to shower Mr Nelson, he reached out to either pinch or touch their breasts or buttocks. He repeatedly made lewd remarks about what his sexual needs were. This unwanted intimate touching certainly disgusted attending care staff who, naturally enough, 'shied' away, giving Mr Nelson instructions from a distance on how to wash his body parts and not doing it for him as he requested.

To make his behaviour worse, when care staff revisited later in the day to supervise his medicines, Mr Nelson was found to be exposed and masturbating in his sitting room for all to see. This caused further embarrassment for care staff and they labelled him a 'randy old man'. He ignored reprimands and made no attempts to stop his activity.

How to implement care that met Mr Nelson's sexual needs posed challenges for the case manager and the clinical nurse consultant. The care staff had already requested that Mr Nelson be transferred to a higher level of care. First there was a need for on-the-spot education for the staff explaining that the unwanted intimate touching and sexual advances, plus Mr Nelson's overt masturbation activities, were not done to shock the care staff, but rather it was behaviour which stemmed from frontotemporal dementia which left him with no inhibitions nor insight into the offensiveness of his behaviour.

Records showed Mr Nelson had been twice divorced and currently had no ongoing partnership. He harboured a lot of anger from his most recent divorce. A daughter from his first marriage visited her father regularly and she was able to give information that her father had been employed as an accountant before his illness forced his retirement. He used to play golf and, being a very social person, spent a lot of time in the clubhouse. His hobby was growing roses. She even made the comment that her father was "a very sexual being, always needing a woman in his life". Mr Nelson was able to point to the high side of the bell curve chart (page 94) and his daughter agreed.

It was obvious from Mr Nelson's sexual history that he had been highly sexually active. To compensate for the current lack of social engagement, companionship and 'comforting touch' in his life, it was thought that remedial massage therapy and engaging the services of a surrogate partner would help. Mr Nelson's financial situation meant he was able to fund a male masseur to give a full body massage twice weekly, as well as twice weekly visits by a surrogate sex worker who came on alternate days to the masseur. The surrogate sex worker was engaged with the proviso that 'safe sex' practices were carried out. Both services were trialled and found to be successful. Each service, in its own way, provided the comforting gratification that was missing in Mr Nelson's life. Mr Nelson's daughter was also invited to be involved in the care planning which was implemented as follows:

• Male masseur attended twice weekly
• Discrete, twice weekly, visits from a female surrogate partner
• Surrogate partner brought Adult DVDs from her service's lending

library exchanging them on a regular basis
- Daughter brought monthly 'adult themed' magazines
- Care staff taught Mr Nelson necessary hygiene skills and set up a special private area for his own 'comfort' private practices
- Daughter compiled a 'life story' book showing the main events and interests in her father's life
- Retirement village management set up an outdoor garden area for Mr Nelson to grow and attend to a rose garden
- Care staff ensured they were aware of any golfing programmes on TV and turned them on for Mr Nelson
- Mr Nelson was encouraged to attend a Living with Memory Loss programme run by the local dementia advisory service.

Visits from both the masseur and the surrogate partner relaxed and de-stressed Mr Nelson. Whilst the sexual activity with the surrogate partner was a very impersonal experience it did provide Mr Nelson with personal gratification and satisfaction that made a difference to his behaviour. It was also a good outcome for the care staff as the intimate touching, sexual advances and overt masturbation were no longer a problem.

The 'life story' book proved very successful. The care staff, during their daily visits, could refer to a specific section as a means of opening communication. Mr Nelson would enthusiastically recall all his golfing achievements or stories during his employment days. The staff, having undergone specific ongoing education programmes to promote understanding of Mr Nelson's behaviour, eventually became quite relaxed in his presence and there was no need to transfer him to another facility.

Dementia and Sexuality

Case study – Mrs Quigley
Parietal lobe dysfunction.
Unfortunately 77-year-old Mrs Quigley, now in the advanced stages of Alzheimer's disease, failed to recognise her husband and sought other male company. She has resided in a dementia specific residential unit for the last three years.
Presenting problem
Agnosia, disrobing and liaising with a co-resident that is not her spouse.

Mr Quigley visited his wife on a daily basis, but she ignored him and was constantly seen disrobing, leaving a trail of clothing in her wake, as she sought frequent physical sexual intimate encounters with a male resident in a room further down the corridor. It was noted that Mrs Quigley and the co-resident were frequently seen caressing each other much to Mr Quigley's dismay.

Mr Quigley explained that this was not a new situation. Intimate relationships had developed previously with other residents. He had already requested his wife be relocated to other sections of the facility on four separate occasions. Unfortunately this was the last available area that Mrs Quigley could be transferred to and Mr Quigley was contemplating applying for transfer to another residential facility. However, he was fearful that no matter where Mrs Quigley would be accommodated she would continue to seek an inappropriate intimate relationship.

On discussion with Mr Quigley, he indicated from the bell curve chart (page 94) that he and his wife were at the high end of the curve as they had always been sexually active up until two years before her admission to the residential unit. For this reason he was disappointed and a little depressed that Mrs Quigley preferred the company of someone else. "After all," he said, "we have been married for 55 years and we have been physically sexually active for 50 of those years."

Mr Quigley confided that he been experiencing erectile dysfunction for those last two years. It had just occurred to him that this might be the reason why Mrs Quigley sought sexual encounters with co-residents. Mr Quigley said his doctor had prescribed a medication that might have helped restore erection, but it had been stopped when he developed a heart problem. It had been suggested that Mr Quigley trial the use of a 'vacuum pump' to help overcome the erectile difficulties. It was explained to him that the penile tissue is placed within the pump so that he pumping action would increase the blood supply to the penile area and achieve the desired erection. Mr Quigley did try this aid with good effect and it was used successfully thereafter.

In the process of collecting Mrs Quigley's life profile it was revealed that she had never worked after their marriage. She had raised two children, a girl now with her own family, and a son and his family living close by, the son being a big support to his father. Mrs Quigley had lived an active community life, becoming president of the parents association at the children's school, and later becoming a volunteer auxiliary worker at the local hospital. She loved knitting and in her earlier days she had a reputation as a good cook.

There were several problems that needed person-centred planning. The first was to help overcome Mrs Quigley's agnosia, not recognising the familiar face of her husband or the intimate relationship they had once shared. Gaining Mr Quigley's consent, he and the unit's management agreed to:

- Display photos connected to courtship, wedding, honeymoon and early marriage days
- Overnight stays for Mr Quigley on a regular basis to rekindle the couple's intimacy
- Suggest Mr Quigley use a lubricating gel as foreplay to overcome any vaginal mucosal dryness or dyspareunia. However, staff were advised that if Mrs Quigley experienced painful intercourse, despite application of gel, medical advice should be sought. Furthermore if Mrs Quigley had any limb discomfort, pillows could be used as a supportive measure and pain relief taken half an hour before any intimate activity
- Unit management to set up an intimate environment:
  - Single accommodation with a double bed or alternatively two beds pushed together
  - Provide a dinner menu, with sumptuous tasting treats and allow wine to be served
  - A 'do not disturb' sign to be on hand when needed to respect the couple's privacy.

Dementia and Sexuality

The next problem to overcome was the disrobing. As was done for Mrs Polanski (refer to Chapter 4), a purchase of a nice silky feeling poncho and kaftan was suggested and made. It was kept on hand, ready to be slipped on when needed. Silk or satin-feeling garments produce a 'sensuous' feel on bare skin, which proved very acceptable and they are easily slipped over the head by staff when needed.

To refocus Mrs Quigley's attention away from her co-resident relationship, a specifically designed plan was implemented as follows:

- A memory box was started filled with family photos, favourite recipes, knitting patterns, badges and certificates of recognition from School and/or hospital volunteer work, as well as other treasured items of interest
- Introduce 'comforting touch' with a daily hand massage
- Trial use of aromatherapy to compliment reminiscence, applying three drops of essential lavender oil in a second daily footbath. Since Mrs Quigley was not allergic to the smell of lavender oil, using it in a footbath was worth a trial period. Care staff were asked to record any changes.

The use of a 'memory box' connected Mrs Quigley to her past life treasures and events. According to Coaten (2001), "multi-sensory triggers, photographs and memorabilia help compensate for different cognitive impairments; objects which can be touched, handled and passed around seem to be particularly important", and these were therefore useful to divert her attention from other behaviours. The hand massage was a useful tool to make contact with Mrs Quigley. It conveyed empathy, letting her know she was not alone, and that her feelings were shared by others.

Implementing all the above plans did have a good outcome for both Mr and Mrs Quigley:

- Mr Quigley withdrew his request to transfer his wife
- Mrs Quigley's relationship with the co-resident was diverted to more personal and comforting gratification with her husband as

a result of Mr Quigley's overnight stays

- Use of the poncho and kaftan overcame the disrobing
- Memorabilia from the memory box helped Mrs Quigley get pleasure out of past events rather than current pursuits
- Alternative sensory therapies helped promote relaxation.

The four different case studies featured in this chapter show how using the steps in the problem solving pathway discussed in the previous chapter, can identify the precise problem and allow planning of individualised interventions. These interventions helped all four people in different ways to refocus their attention to more appropriate and comforting stimuli by tapping into past interests, memories and skills of each individual person. It gave them back their self-worth and helped increase their well-being.

CHAPTER NINE

Facilitating Change

The focus of this final chapter will be on ways in which change can be facilitated. Its aim is to show how negative reactive approaches can be converted into more positive proactive courses of action to support a person living with dementia maintain their sexuality in a way that will enhance their quality of living.

'For things to change, we must change. For things to get better, we must get better'

Heidi Wills

Dementia and Sexuality

Facilitating change in a way that will satisfy a person living with dementia's sexual desires and drives is needed to maintain dignity and well being, and will always be a challenging and complex task for care staff.

The change process is complex because attitudes influence how care staff approach the situation. Some members of staff feel uncomfortable with the people in their care overtly seeking sexual fulfillment and they perceive it as a problem. This negativity stems from the fact that some care staff, as discussed in Chapter 2, have difficulty contemplating anyone older having sexual relationships, especially if they have a diagnosis of dementia.

Breaking down attitudinal barriers is a long process. A good start to breaching these barriers is to remind the staff that the people in their care were once young (perhaps like the staff are now), and have just grown older. It is always a good thought provoking question to ask staff if they think they will still be sexually active when they are 70 years old. The responses are usually varied, but on average, most would still like to think they could continue their sexual activity beyond their three score years and ten, even if they have dementia.

Ongoing education programmes are required to facilitate an appreciation and sensitivity that human beings, whatever the age or disability, have sexually driven needs and desires which have "long been woven into the tapestry of human existence" (Bancroft, 2009). These sexually driven needs should be of prime consideration when planning care and support and privacy should be given to fulfill this natural part of life.

Projecting positive images of aged people who are Nobel Prize winners or are contributing to society, science and sport for example, can help debunk any negative attitudes that might remain. Admittedly these people used as examples may not have dementia, but being positive about people who are older helps reinforce the point that people living with dementia still have qualities and attributes that make them unique in their own individual way.

Health education about dementia can make all the difference for staff in understanding fully a person's progression through the stages of dementia and, therefore, the reasons for the marked changes in behaviour. For example, it is helpful to know that those with frontal or temporal lobe involvement are the people most likely to show the most anti-social behaviour, although other lobes of the brain affected by the dementia process can contribute to disinhibited behaviour (Kamel *et al* 2004). It is essential that staff keep in mind that the primary carer needs access to dementia information as well, and they will need to be advised where support groups can be found. Greater understanding helps the primary carer to appreciate and work through the behavioural changes as they arise.

Whilst increasing or reinforcing background knowledge will help experienced care staff to facilitate change to proactive problem solving approaches, many of the less experienced staff might still remain negatively reactive. It is important, therefore, for education to take account of all the varying knowledge, skill levels and experience of staff involved.

This approach is backed by Ward *et al*'s (2005) research in aged care facilities which found that "older carers reported the perception that younger and less experienced female staff found it more difficult to cope with sexual advances from a resident, echoing the findings of existing studies that have highlighted the distress that such incidents can cause and their potentially detrimental impact upon carer/caree relationships" (Archibald, 2001, 2002; Barnes, 2001). It does need to be emphasized that if continual inappropriate behaviour stresses younger staff, or a staff member has suffered previous sexual exploitation in any form that reignites haunting memories, it is advisable for the staff member to be reassigned to another person's care (refer to Chapter 1). Education can be an essential catalyst to dispel any homophobic negativity, replacing it with "an understanding of the diverse nature of the human race and an appreciation of the 'uniqueness' of every individual" (Kuhn, 2002). Education can also be used to help promote, as Barrett (2009) explains, "an understanding that the grief and loss involved in having a same-sex partner with dementia is no less than that experienced by heterosexual couples".

Dementia and Sexuality

Price (2009) advises, "because of the complexity of sexuality and the part played by life history and human relationships within it, care prescription is difficult. There are no right ways to proceed, only better ways to understand and respect. Understanding and respect begins with a willingness to think afresh about our own experiences of and attitudes towards sexuality".

Case Study – Mrs Peterson
Vascular Dementia.
80 years of age, Mrs Peterson had recently been transferred from an acute care setting to a high dependency residential care facility.
Presenting problem
Masturbating with a banana.

Mrs Peterson had a long history of transient ischaemic attacks (TIAs), damaging her brain and resulting in her current diagnosis of vascular dementia. More recently she had suffered a dense stroke which paralysed the left side of her body. Subsequently the staff reported they had observed Mrs Peterson's repeatedly and overtly masturbating with a banana. This action made staff very disdainful. Mrs Peterson was labeled 'a dirty old woman'. The problem was referred to a clinical nurse consultant to provide a solution.

On assessment the pungent odour that came from Mrs Peterson's vagina alerted the nurse consultant to the fact that she was suffering from an undetected gross vaginitis. This odour might have indicated the underlying problem earlier, but unfortunately staff put it down to urinary incontinence. During the clinical education process following the assessment, it was pointed out that if staff had been more diligent and carried out a meticulous assessment, especially looking at Mrs Peterson's genital area, while helping with her personal hygiene including showering, toileting and dressing, they would have realised she was using the banana to relieve itching due to a serious vaginal thrush infection and it was not masturbation at all. Mrs Peterson

Taking these processes into account, together with any life-programming religious or cultural teachings, care staff have to be open-minded and non-judgmental so that their own beliefs/values do not influence their duty of care (Hajjar *et al*, 2004; Brock *et al*, 2007). Problems should not be allowed to arise simply because of individual opinions or assumptions that are hastily made without meticulous assessment, as shown by two case studies included here.

had been prevented by a stroke-resultant dysarthric speech problem from telling the staff about her discomfort and pain.

A vaginal swab was taken and the results confirmed the presence of gross vaginitis. Her doctor was advised and treatment prescribed. This treatment not only cured the vaginitis but Mrs Peterson's urinary incontinence, and the 'masturbation'.

Mrs Peterson's case study was a good example of how negative attitudes can be changed around to achieve a positive outcome. Using on-the-spot education and reference to the old adage "things are not always what they seem", care staff were shown that Mrs Peterson's 'scratching' actions had been misconstrued as anti-social behaviour when in actual fact they were not. Observations made without meticulous assessment can be misleading and assumptions can be made that can label a person wrongly – sometimes for life.

With the change in attitude to Mrs Peterson came a proactive approach designed to restore dignity as well as enhance her physical and emotional comfort. Firstly, time was taken over her genital cleanliness – a precautionary measure to prevent recurrence of the vaginitis. Thereafter a remedial masseur was engaged, with Mrs Peterson's permission, to relax her aching body; in particular her hemiplegic limbs, shoulder and hands. A long narrow 'comfort' pillow was used at night, supporting the left side of her body and providing a softness to cuddle up to. She was included in the social activities within the facility and attended a weekly hairdressing appointment, enhancing her body image and self-respect. This re-establishment of her identity as a vibrant sensuous person, no longer labeled 'a dirty old woman,' made a huge difference to her well-being and quality of living.

Dementia and Sexuality

Case study – Mr Rawson
Combination of both Alzheimer's and vascular dementia.
75 years of age, Mr Rawson had been recently diagnosed and was currently residing in a transitional hospital unit awaiting placement in a dementia specific unit.
Presenting problem
Recurrent visual hallucinations that disturbed his sleep.

The care staff on night duty reported that Mr Rawson was up several times each night, anxiously telling the staff that he had to "find places to accommodate his nude ladies". He exhibited aggressive behaviour when the care staff tried to put him back to bed and would continually refer to his nude ladies as "beautiful creatures", and they needed to be "put under a spotlight to show off their beauty". Mr Rawson's behaviour was put down to the visual hallucinations which staff knew were frequently seen in Dementia with Lewy bodies, even though Mr Rawson was diagnosed with a mixed type of dementia. Unfortunately care staff had jumped to the conclusion that Mr Rawson had probably been the owner of a brothel and they had labeled him as a 'randy old man', stating how they "pitied his poor wife!".

The situation was referred to a clinical nurse consult to find a solution. The nurse consultant welcomed the opportunity to facilitate attitudinal change by educating staff in the benefits and use of the problem solving pathway described in Chapter 7. Change will come about when care staff are taught not to react negatively to unusual or challenging behaviour but to understand

The two case studies show the importance of education and mentoring, equipping staff with the skills and knowledge they might need in similar situations. Pointon (2008) explains "gaining better knowledge and understanding of the factors influencing behaviours and emotions transforms attitudes and fosters greater sensitivity, thoughtfulness and empathy towards the individuals". For both Mrs Peterson and Mr Rawson this knowledge contributed to much better staff-resident interactions, and helped in the way the person-centred care plans were implemented.

the origins of it by asking questions such as "tell me what you see" and "who are these beautiful ladies?" Starting any questioning with a 'why' is usually not recommended as the person with dementia does not know 'why' and may become agitated and confabulate an answer. Questioning should generally be led with 'who', 'what', where' and 'how'. As Feil (1993) explains "The 'whys' of the world are not important any more".

Attitudes changed dramatically when staff were included in a history gathering interview with Mr Rawson's wife. Mrs Rawson revealed that her husband had been a respected curator of a regional art gallery before he retired. She stated, "up until the dementia process interfered with my husband's intellectual functioning he was a highly regarded art critic, writing for prominent newspapers." This case provided another example of 'things not being what they seem'. What was perceived as hallucinatory deviant behaviour was, in actual fact, due to Mr Rawson's confusional state. His mind had taken him back into his familiar, pleasurable but responsible role of displaying revered artistic paintings and placing his nude statues where they could be seen to best advantage.

A big change in Mr Rawson's behaviour, as well as the attitude of care staff, resulted when Mrs Rawson responded to the request to bring in her husband's collection of classical art books. Staff reported that Mr Rawson was content sitting and turning the pages of his art books; reconnecting, in his mind's eye, to the elegance of his art world. The night staff also reported that he now slept well and his night-time wanderings were a thing of the past.

Another good way to bring about change is to have an open forum where care staff can freely express their attitudes and concerns relating to sexual issues encountered in their workplace (Hajjar *et al*, 2004). Open debate can bring a lot of 'burning' issues to the surface that can be worked through within the group. Ward *et al* (2005) found "there is a clear requirement to move beyond a focus upon sexual expression as a problem within care, to consider strategies that may facilitate and enhance this aspect of the lives of people with dementia residing in care".

Dementia and Sexuality

In any service – be it acute, community or residential – that is involved in a person's care, facilitating change needs to start at the top management level. Such support may be needed to ensure policies are put in place that enable both a person's life profile and sexual history to be "a routine part of every admission assessment" (Kamel *et al*, 2004). "Sexual questions should not be preceded by an apology, suggesting that they are inappropriate or embarrassing, but conducted in a forthright and dignified manner."

Having personal information documented in the person's record notes could prevent attitudinal barriers developing because the staff should be able to anticipate an individual's sexually-centred needs and plan care accordingly. Records need to identify the particular way a person living with dementia likes to express the intricacies of their sexuality, such as:

- Sensuality: for example dress, grooming and fragrance
- Identity: important life experiences and interests indicating that the person still remains a sexual human being
- Levels of intimacy: what levels will keep the person connected and meaningfully occupied with social engagement, interaction, friendship and closeness with others?

Obtaining details of a person's sexual orientation during the admission process (as discussed in Chapter 2) is important. It will identify the person responsible for providing any additional information needed, or for conjoint decision making, and will avoid any 'invisibility' that may cause a long standing partner stress or frustration.

With managerial approval, changes can be facilitated in residential care by using a proactive approach to maintaining an older person's level of 'intimacy'. Spouse/partner separation trauma can be prevented by inviting and encouraging a spouse or partner to stay overnight in a private room within the residential facility. Beds can to be pushed together and 'do not disturb' signs placed on the door. "The preservation of self-identity," as noted by the Australian National Ageing Research Institute (2002), "may be one of the most important needs of older people, particularly those who are institutionalised." Making a 'homelike' environment conducive to intimate encounters offers couples "an opportunity of lying next to each other, stroking, touching, caressing and of being held" according to Greengross *et al* (1989). This level of intimacy, bringing its own rewards of pleasurable and comforting gratification can, for some couples, be more important than the genital excitement of a sexual penetrative relationship (Greengross, 1989).

A proactive approach needs to show sensitivity and appreciate that some couples may still long for the pleasure of shared physical intimacy. Greengross *et al* (1989) explain, "The naked exposure of intercourse is not only physical but sometimes a deep emotional nakedness as well between two people." Physical intercourse has further advantages, it can ward off impotence for men and maintain vaginal lubrication for women, but whatever the level of intimacy shared it offers comforting reassurance and an opportunity to demonstrate affection and emotional connection.

Whilst many care staff will support this proactive approach there are others who will still view it negatively. This could include a concern that either one or both of a couple might fall from the bed. This argument becomes invalid with the use of modern beds with an in-built adjustable bed height mechanism which can, if necessary, lower the bed to floor level.

Throughout this chapter, it has been demonstrated that the challenges and complexities of facilitating change can be overcome by education. Education is the key to understanding and promoting a positive knowledge base, plus sensitivity that the person living with dementia is a vibrant sexual person.

A proactive approach, as shown in the two case studies, facilitates change and makes a difference to how residential care can be delivered. Management has a responsibility to ensure life and sexual histories become a routine part of the admission process (Kamel *et al*, 2004) because this pre-empts individuals having to express their sexual needs perhaps inappropriately, and allows staff to plan requirements and care from the start in a way that will enrich the well-being and quality of living for the person living with dementia.

Dementia and Sexuality: a Rose that Never Wilts

This chapter will explore the origins of the negative social prejudices surrounding sexuality and people living with dementia. It will lay to rest a lot of myths and misconceptions that arise for care staff when faced with what is perceived as inappropriate sexual behaviour.

'People from a planet without flowers would think we must be mad with joy the whole time to have such things about us'

Dame Iris Murdoch CBE

Dementia and Sexuality

Reflecting on the concept of a rosebud representing 'sexuality', with its beautiful petals and many parts, gives the reader a chance to appreciate that there is more to sexuality than just a physical act. The rosebud orchestrates its petals to unfurl their separate intricate contents; sensuality, identity, level of intimacy, life's programming and reproduction. This orchestration can be compared to an orchestral conductor making the most of the various sections of an orchestra showing that each musical instrument, whilst different, has an important part to play, similar to the rose petals, interacting and in harmony with one another. However if a musical note is played off key the whole harmony is disrupted as it is when sexual exploitation emerges to expose the darker thorny side of the rose concept.

As highlighted by all the case studies in this book, human sexuality remains a constant need in the lives of older people; especially those living with dementia. Humans are sexual beings in one way or another and will be until the day they die (Hajjar *et al*, 2004). There may be variations in occurrence, intensity and expression but their desire for affectionate, close, comforting, intimate relationships remains.

Unfortunately, dementia can have an impact and influence on the way some people inappropriately express their sexuality. More often than not this behaviour, together with care staff's lack of understanding and skills, results in a build-up of negativity. Consequently the behaviour is perceived as a problem. Remember too that often the negativity can be complicated by each staff member's own life programming or possible past experience of sexual exploitation.

However, education is the foundation to facilitate changes in care staff's attitudes, giving them a knowledge base and the skills required to support the individual with dementia to express their sexuality in the appropriate way to fulfill their needs. It is also invaluable in helping avoid ethical dilemmas, and promoting understanding of the underlying processes which may result in a dilemma.

It is imperative that care staff be taught to follow the steps within the problem solving pathway to uncover the reason for the person living with dementia's behaviour and the problems associated with it. This proactive problem solving approach gives a real opportunity to make a difference by changing a perceived problem situation into a desirable outcome (Rusbult, 2001). Life enhancing strategies to complement the need for sensuality, appropriate levels of intimacy and identity can be implemented on a person centred basis to help reconnect the person to their past experiences, pleasures and sexual gratification. In this way a person's dignity, well being and quality of living will be restored and maintained.

As a member of a care staff team we each need to appreciate that the need for sexuality is planted deep in every human being. It is a birth to death continuum. So whatever the age, disability or level of dementia, sexuality – as conceptualized as a rose throughout this book, in one form or another – unlike a real rose, never wilts!

Finally, as the author, I hope that all those who have read this book have gained an increased knowledge, understanding, sensitivity and respect for those wishing to continue their sexual activity into their later years, including those with a diagnosis of dementia. I would like to conclude with a second quote from the well-remembered Booker Prize-winning author and philosopher, Dame Iris Murdoch, who in her later years lived with dementia:

"We can only learn to love by loving"

References

Alzheimer's Australia, *What is Dementia?* Fact Sheet, published by Alzheimer's Australia, 2005

Alzheimer's Australia, Victoria, *Dementia – sexuality and intimacy – Fact Sheet,* 2008, *www.betterhealth.vic.gov.au,*

Annon, J, *The PLISSIT model: a proposed conceptual scheme for the behavioural treatment of sexual problems,* 1976, Journal of Sex Education Therapy, 2,1-15

Archibald, C, *Residential sexual expression and the key worker relationship: An unspoken stress in residential care park?* 2001, Practice, 13 (1), P.5-12. . Cited in Ward, et.al., *A kiss is still a kiss –The construction of sexuality in dementia care.* 2005, Dementia SAGE Publications 4(1) 49-72

Archibald, C, *Sexuality and dementia in residential care – whose responsibility?* 2002, Sexual and Relationship Therapy, 17(3),P. 301-309. Cited in Ward, et.al. *A kiss is still a kiss –The construction of sexuality in dementia care.* 2005, Dementia SAGE Publications 4(1) 49-72

Archibald, C, *Sexuality & Dementia. A guide for all staff working with people with dementia,* 2005, The Dementia Services Development Centre, Stirling

Archibald, C, *Sexuality and dementia: the role dementia plays when sexual expression becomes a component of residential care work* 2003 Alzheimer's care quarterly. 4 (2), April/June. 137-148

Arnell, V., *Fact Sheet: How the Brain Works: An Analogy,* in The Dementia Educator, Vol1.No.1. August 1997 P.6-7

Attorney General's Department of NSW, *Capacity Toolkit... information for government and community workers, professionals, families and carers in New South Wales.* 2009, ecoDesign ecoPrint, Wolli Creek, Sydney, Section 3, Ch.2, P32.

Bailey, R., *Limbic System,* About.com.Biology, 1/1/2010, http://biology.about.com/od/anatomy/a/aa042205a.htm

Baines, P, *Nurturing the Heart: creativity, art therapy and dementia,* 2007, Australian Government Initiative Publication. No. 3 in the Quality Dementia Care Series

Bancroft, J, *Introduction,,* cited in *Human Sexuality and its Problems,* 2009, Churchill Livingston, Elsevier, Edinburgh, 3rd Ed. Ch. 1 P1.

Bancroft, J, *Sexual Arousal and Response: The Psychosomatic Cycle.* cited in *Human Sexuality and its Problems,* 2009, Churchill Livingston, Elsevier, Edinburgh, 3rd Ed. Chapter 4 P55-57

Banks, S, *Tips for music at home,* 2009, www.alzheimers.org.au

Barnes, I, *Sexuality and cognitive impairment in long-term care.* 2001, Canadian Nursing Home,12 (3),P.5-15. . Cited in Ward, et.al., *A kiss is still a kiss –The construction of sexuality in dementia care.* 2005, Dementia SAGE Publications 4(1) 49-72

Barrett, C, Harrison J & Kent J., *Permission to speak – Determining strategies* towards the development of gay, lesbian, bisexual, transgender and intersex friendly aged care services in Victoria. 2009, Matrix Guild Victoria Inc. P. 1, 57,72

Benson, K, Nursing home staff sacked tor alleged sexual abuse, 2008, reported in Sydney Morning Herald, John Fairfax Publications Pty. Ltd. Oct. 22 P. 1.

Berger, R.M., The unseen minority: older gays and lesbian, 1982, Social Work, 27(3) 236-42, cited in Mackenzie, J. 2009, Working with lesbian and gay people with dementia, 2009, Journal of Dementia Care, Vol. 17 No. 6 P. 17-19

Birch, H, It is not just about sex! Dementia, Lesbians and Gay Men, 2009, National Library Australia, collection catalogue. nia.gov.au/Record4509096

Blanch, M and Collier, M, There's more to Sexuality....teaching notes, 1990, Family Planning Association of New South Wales, Ashfield NSW, P.3 - 4

Boeree, C.G., The Emotional Nervous System: The Limbic System, 7/1/2010, http://webspace.ship.edu/cgboer/limbicsystem.html

Briggs, J, Management of Constipation in Older Adults, The Joanna Briggs Institute Evidence Based Practice Information Sheet, 1999.Revised Feb. 2004

Bright, R, Music Therapy and the Dementias: Improving the Quality of Life, 1997. 2nd. Ed. St. Louis, MMB

Brock L.J. & Jennings, G. , Sexuality and Intimacy, 2007, In: Blackburn, J.A. Dulmus, C.N., (eds) Handbook of Gerontology: Evidence Approaches to Theory, Practice and Policy, John Wiley & Sons, New Jersey, pp. 244-68. cited in Nay, R., & Garratt, S. Older People, Issues and Innovations in Care, 2009, , Churchill Livingston Elsevier, Sydney 3rd. Ed. Ch.17 P. 295, 303

Brucsia, K, Tips for music at home, , 2009, www.alzheimers.org.au

Burns, P., A Carer's Personal Journey over Time, 2010, Time for Dementia Hawker Publications. London, Ch. 5P. 65-66

Bush, E., The Use of Human Touch to Improve the Well-Being of Older Adults, 2001, Journal of Holistic Nursing. Vol.19 No.3 Sept-. P.256-270

Cloud, G.C., Browne, R., Salooja N. et al, Newly diagnosed HIV infection in an octogenarian: the elderly are not 'immune' 2003, Age and Ageing, 32 (3)P. 353-4, cited in Nay, R & Garratt, S. Older people: Issues and Innovations in Care, 2009, Churchill Livingston Elsevier, Sydney 3rd Ed. Ch.17. P.303,

Coaten, R., Exploring reminiscence through dance and movement, 2001, Journal of Dementia Care Sept/Oct, P.19-21

Creasey, H., Understanding the Brain and Behaviour, Alzheimer's Australia; An Australian Government Initiative: Summer Hill Media, 2004

Department of Constitutional Affairs (2007) Mental Capacity Act 2005 Code of Practice. London Stationary Office, http://www.opsi.gov.uk/acts/ acts2005/related/ukpgacop_20050009_en.pdf

Davis S. & Taylor, B., From PLISSIT to exPLISSIT, 2006. Cited in http://metaot.com/blog/sexuality-and-health care, May 2009.

Douglas, S., James I. & Ballard, C., Non-pharmacological interventions in dementia, 2004, Advances in Psychiatric Treatment, Vol.10.171-179

Doheny, K., 10 Surprising Health Benefits of Sex, 2010, WebMD, Better information, Better health, http://www.webmd.com/sex- relationships/features/10-surprising-health-benefits-of-sex, February 6

Dementia and Sexuality

Ellis, S.R. & Morrison, T.G., *Sterotypes of ageing:messages promoted by age-specific paper birthday cards available in Canada,* 2005 citied in Nay, *et al, Sexuality: from stigma, stereotypes and secrecy to coming out, communication and choice,* 2007,The International Journal of Older People Nursing , Blackwell Publishing Ltd. 2,76-80

Feil, N., *Validation Therapy,* 1972, cited in Morton, I, 1999, *Person centred approaches to dementia care, Winslow Press, Boston.*
Feil, N., *The Validation Breakthrough, Simple Techniques for Communication with People with Alzheimer's-Type Dementia,* 1993, MacLennan & Petty Pty. Limited, Artarmon.
Feinberg School of Medicine, *What is frontotemporal dementia?* North Western University in http://www.brain.northwestern.edu/mdad/frontal.html 4/7/2009

Greengross, W, & Greengross S., *Living, Loving & Ageing.... Sexual and Person Relationships in Later Life,*1989, Ebenezer Baylis & Son Ltd, Worcester, Ch. 7. P.81-92
Griffiths, E.R. and Lemberg.S, *Sexuality ad the Person with Traumatic Brain Injury - a guide for families,* 1993, F.A. Davis, Philadelphia
Guardianship Tribunal NSW, *Information – 'person responsible'* 2009, Fact Sheet Page 1. www.gt.nsw.au

Haddad,P & Benbow S, *Sexual Problems Associated with Dementia: Part 2 Aetiology, assessment and treatment.* Internat.J. Geriatric Psych.1993; 8:631-637 Cited in Hashmi, F.H. *et al:* Sexually Disinhibited Behavior in Cognitively Impaired Elderly: http://www.clinicalgeriatrics.com/article/ 1022. 4/09/2007
Hajjar, R.R. & Kamel, H.K. , *Sexuality in Nursing Home, Part 1: Attitudes and Barriers to Sexual Expression ,* 2004, Journal American Medical Directors Association,P543-547
Harris, P.B , *Intimacy, Sexuality and Early-Stage Dementia: The Changing Marital Relationship,* 2009, Alzheimer's Care Today , 10(2) P. 63-77
Hashmi, F. H' Krady,A.I. Qayum, F & Grossberg, G.T., *Sexually Disinhibited Behaviour in Cognitively Impaired Elderly:* http://www.clinicalgeriatrics.com/article/1022. 4/09/2007
Hillman ,J., *Knowledge and Attitudes about HIV/AIDS, among community-living elder women re-examining issues of age and gender.* 2007, Journal of Women and Ageing 19: (3/4):53-67, cited in Nay, R & Garratt, S. *Older people: Issues and Innovations in Care,* 2009, , Churchill Livingston Elsevier, Sydney 3rd Ed. Ch.17. P.302/303
Holt, F.E, Birks, T.P.H, Thorgrimsen,L.M., Spector, A.E., Wiles, A., & Orrel,M , *Aroma therapy for dementia (Review),* 2009, The Cochrane Collaboration, John Wiley & Sons, Ltd.
Huffstetler, B, *Sexuality in older adults: a deconstructivist perspective,* 2006, Adultspan 5 (1):4-14 cited in Nay, R & Garratt, S. *Older people: Issues and Innovations in Care,* 2009, Churchill Livingston Elsevier, Sydney , 3rd Ed. Ch.17. P.298,

Jamieson, T, *Nursing home accused of elderly abuse,* 1999, Sydney Morning Herald, Jan 30 P. 4. John Fairfax Publications Pty. Ltd.

Jeter , L. , *Elder abuse prevention association policy statement,* 2008, cited in *Nursing home staff sacked for alleged sexual abuse,* 2008, reported in Sydney Morning Herald,. John Fairfax Publications Pty. Ltd. Oct.22 P.1

Johnson, G..S. Jnr, *About Brain Injury: A guide to brain anatomy, function and symptoms,* cited in http://www.com/brain function.html, Jul. 2009

Kamel, H.K. & Hajjar, R.R., *Sexuality in the Nursing Home, Part 2: Managing Abnormal Behavior – Legal and Ethical Issues,* 2004, Journal American Medical Directors Association P549-552

Kastenbaum, R., *Growing Old: Years of Fulfillment,* 1979, Harper & Rowe Publishers, New York, Ch. 2, P. 22,

Kitwood, T &Brendin, K, *Towards a Theory of Dementia Care: Personhood and Wellbeing,* 1992, Ageing Society,12:269-287

Knocker, S, *The whole of me: meeting the needs of older lesbians, gay men and bisexuals living in care homes and extra care housing. A Resource pack.* 2006, Age Concern, London. Cited in Archibald, C. *Gay and lesbian issues: learning on the (research) job* 2006, Journal of Dementia Care July/August P 21-23

Kuhn, D., *Intimacy, Sexuality ad Residents with Dementia,2002,* Alzheimer's Care Quarterly 2003 Aspen Publishers Inc. 3 (2):165-176,

Lemieux, L., Kaiser, S., Pereira, J & Meadows, L.M. , *Sexuality in palliative care: patient perspective.* 2004. In Bauer, M. 2007,The International Journal of Older People Nursing 2,63-68, Blackwell Publishing Ltd.

Lezah, M. D., *Behavioural Geography of the Brain* cited in *Neuropsychological Assessment,* 1995, Oxford University Press Inc. New York 3rd ed. Chapter 3, P. 73, 81-83

Lishman, W.A, *Toxic Disorders in Organic Psychiatry: The Psychological Consequences of Cerebral Disorders,* 1 2nd ed. Oxford, Blackwell;1987: 508-544 Cited in Hashmi, F.H. *et al:* Sexually Disinhibited Behavior in Cognitively Impaired Elderly: http://www.clinicalgeriatrics.com/article/1022. 4/09/2007

McAuliffe, L, Bauer, M & Nay, R, *Barriers to the expression of sexuality in the older person: the role of the health professional,* 2007 , The International Journal of Older People Nursing , Blackwell Publishing Ltd.2,69-75

McCreadie, C. & Penhale, B., *Abuse of Older People,* 2006 cited in Redfern, S. J. & Ross F.M. *Nursing Older People,* 2006, Churchill Livingstone Elsevier, Edinburgh. 4th Ed. Ch. 32, P.691

Mackenzie, J, *Working with lesbian and gay people with dementia,* 2009, Journal of Dementia Care, Nov./ Dec. Vol. 17 No. 6 P. 17-19

Manthorpe, J, *Nearest and Dearest? The neglect of lesbians in caring relationships.* 2003 British Journal of Social Work 33 753-68. Cited in Mackenzie, J. 2009, *Working with lesbian and gay people with dementia,* 2009, Journal of Dementia Care, Nov./Dec. Vol. 17 No. 6 P. 17-19

Macquarie Concise Dictionary, 3rd. ed., 2006, The Macquarie Library Pty. Ltd. Sydney

Dementia and Sexuality

Masters, W & Johnson, V, *The Human Sexual Response,* 1966, cited in Benuto, L, 10/8/2009 The Sexual Response Cycle: A Historical Perspective on the Classification of Sexual Disorders http://www.mentalhelp.net/poc/view_doc.php?type=doc&id=29694&cn=10

Maugham, W. Somerset, Cited in Greengross *et al; In Living, Loving & Ageing.... Sexual and Person Relationships in Later Life,*1989, Ebenezer Baylis & Son Ltd, Worcester, Ch. 9. P.113

MedlinePlus Medical Encyclopedia Image, *The Limbic System,* updated 29/3 2009, http://www.nlm.nih.gov/medlineplus/ency/imagepages/19244.htm

Metherell, M, *New checks designed to target aged care abuses,* 2006, reported in Sydney Morning Herald, John Fairfax Publications Pty. Ltd. Apr. 11, P.3

Metzger, E & Gillick, M, *Ethics Corner: Cases from the Hebrew Rehabilitation Center for Ages – Sex in the Facility,* 2002, JAMDA – Nov.-Dec. P. 390-392

Minichiello V., Ackling, S., Bourne, C & Plummer, D., *Sexuality, sexual intimacy and sexual health in later life* 2005, cited in Bauer, M *et al* 2007 The International Journal of Older People Nursing Blackwell Publishing Ltd.2,63-68,

Moss, B.F. & Schwebel, A.I, *Defining intimacy in romantic relationships.* Family Relationships, 1993;42(1):31-37. Cited in Kuhn. D *Intimacy, Sexuality ad Residents with Dementia,* Alzheimer's Care Quarterly 2003(2):165-176, Aspen Publishers Inc.

National Ageing Research Institute, *The Wellness Project: Promoting Older People's Sexual Health, National Ageing Research Institute, Melbourne. Online: Available www.mednwh.unimelb.edu.au/research/service_rae.htm,* cited in Nay, R., & Garratt, S. *Older People, Issues and Innovations in Care,* 2009, Churchill Livingston Elsevier, Sydney, 3rd. Ed. Ch.17, P. 297

Nay, R , *Sexuality and older people.* cited in *Nursing Older People: Issues and Innovation,* 2004, Cited in Nay, R & Garratt S., Churchill Livingston, Elsevier, Marrickville, NSW 2nd ed. Ch. 17 pp. 276-288

Nay, R, McAuliffe, L. & Bauer, M, *Sexuality: from stigma, stereotypes and secrecy to coming out, communication and choice,* 2007,The International Journal of Older People Nursing Blackwell Publishing Ltd. 2,76-80,

Nuffield Council on bioethics (2009) Dementia Ethical Issues London, www.nuffieldbioethics.org

O'Neill, M., *Lateline – Abuse in Nursing Homes Scandal,* Australian Broadcasting Corporation. 2006, Sydney Feb. 27 p.1. cited in http://proquest.umi.com/pqdweb?index=4&sid=2& srchmode=2&vubst=PROD&fmt

Ozanne, E., Naughtin, G., Kurrle, S. & Koch, S., *Intervention in a situation of elder abuse and neglect,* cited in Nay, R., & Garratt, S. *Older People, Issues and Innovations in Care,* 2009, Churchill Livingston Elsevier, Sydney 3rd. Ed. Ch.18 P. 31,

Phair, Lynne, MA BSc(Hons) Nursing, RGN, RMN DPNS IP Clinical Advisor, Safeguarding Vulnerable groups Act team, Department of Health, London.

Pointon, B, *Forward,* cited in Stokes, G. *And Still the Music Plays: Stories of people with dementia,* 2009, Hawker Publications, London P.5

Price, E, *Pride or Prejudice? Gay men, lesbians and dementia*. 2008 British Journal of Social Work 38 (7)1 337-52

Rheaume, C. & Mitty, E, *Sexuality and Intimacy in Older Adults*, 2008, Geriatric Nursing, Mosby Inc.Vol.29, No 5, P.342 -349,

Rusbult, C., *Thinking Skills & Problem-Solving Methods in education*, 2001, cited July 2009 in http://www.asa3.org/ASA/education/think/methods.htm

Scottish Government (2007) Adults with incapacity (Scotland Act) Code of Practice, http://www.scotland.gov.uk/Publications/2008/03/20114619/0

Sherman, B, *Sex, Intimacy and Aged Care*, 1998, Melbourne, ACER Press, P. 91, cited in Harris, P. B., *Intimacy, Sexuality and Early-Stage Dementia: The Changing Marital Relationship*, 2009, Alzheimer's Care Today , 10(2) P. 63-77

Staunton, P & Chiarella, M, *Nursing and the Law* 2008, Churchill Livingston, Elsevier, Sydney 6th ed. Ch.4 P. 126-133,

Van Kerrebroeck, P. Abrams, P, Chalkin D et.al., *The standardisation of terminology in nocturia: Report from the standardisation subcommittee of the International Continence Society*, 2002, Neuroural Urodynam 21:179-183

Van Wagner, K, The Anatomy of the Bran: The Thalamus, 7/1/2010 http://psychology.about.com/od/biopsychology/ss/brainstructure_6.htm

Verity, J, *Activities and Therapies*, 2010, http://www.dementiacareaustralia.com/index.php/activities-and-therapies.html February 14

Verity, J, *Doll Therapy*, 2010, http://www.dementiacareaustralia.com/index.php/doll-therapy. html Feb14

Wallace, N, *Sacking in Nursing Scandal, 2008*, reported in Sydney Morning Herald, John Fairfax Publications Pty. Ltd. Oct. 31, P. 2,

Ward R, Vass A, Aggarwal N, Garfield C. & Cybyk.B, *A kiss is still a kiss –The construction of sexuality in dementia care.* 2005, Dementia SAGE Publications 4(1) 49-72

Wesley, Uniting Care, *Culture and sexuality/gender identity*, 2009, Jun.24. http://www.ucwesleyadelaide.org.au/bfriend/cald_culture_and_sexuality.htm

White, E., *Time to Reflect*, In Gilliard, J and Marshall, M (Ed) 2010, Time for Dementia, Hawker Publications. London, Ch. 5. P 74

World Health Organisation (WHO), *Sexual Health document series; Working Definitions*, 2006 Ch.3 P5. http://www.int/reproductivehealth/topics/gender_rights/defining_sexual_health

Williams, K, *Capacity – when can a person make their own decisions?* 2009, Nursing Review, September, P12-13, www.nursingreview.com.au